Democratic Vistas

The

IOWA WHITMAN SERIES

Ed Folsom, series editor

Democratic Vistas

THE ORIGINAL EDITION IN FACSIMILE

by Walt Whitman

EDITED BY ED FOLSOM

UNIVERSITY OF IOWA PRESS, IOWA CITY

University of Iowa Press, Iowa City 52242
Copyright © 2010 by the University of Iowa Press
www.uiowapress.org
Printed in the United States of America
Design by Richard Hendel

The University of Iowa Press is a member of Green Press Initiative
and is committed to preserving natural resources.

Printed on acid-free paper

Library of Congress Cataloging-in-Publication Data
Whitman, Walt, 1819–1892.
Democratic vistas: the original edition in facsimile /
by Walt Whitman; edited by Ed Folsom.
p.   cm. — (The Iowa Whitman series, ISSN 1556-5610)
Includes bibliography of works about Democratic vistas.
ISBN-13: 978-1-58729-870-7 (pbk.) ISBN-10: 1-58729-870-8 (pbk.)
1. United States — Politics and government — 1869–1877.
2. Whitman, Walt, 1819–1892 — Political and social views.
3. Whitman, Walt, 1819–1892. Democratic vistas.
I. Folsom, Ed, 1947–   II. Title.
PS3213.A2F65   2010
814'.3 — dc22   2009036883

{ Contents }

{ Acknowledgments }

I have learned a great deal over the years about Whitman from my friends and colleagues in the Whitman scholarly community, and I thank them all. Ken Price, Ted Genoways, Jerry Loving, Betsy Erkkila, and Alan Trachtenberg have been particularly influential in my reading of *Democratic Vistas*, as has my former student and now colleague Luke Mancuso. My research assistant and former Whitman seminar participant, Heidi Bean, has been an immense help with the notes for this volume, many of which she drafted. I am grateful to the students in my Whitman seminar over many years for their insights into *Democratic Vistas*, including Sam Graber, Matt Miller, Blake Bronson-Bartlett, and Eric Conrad.

Some of the material from the introduction to this volume appeared in different forms in various publications. I thank Donald D. Kummings and J. R. LeMaster for giving me the opportunity to articulate what I took to be Whitman's conceptions of democracy for *Walt Whitman: An Encyclopedia* (New York: Garland, 1996); David Reynolds for giving me the opportunity to work out my views about Whitman and his attitudes toward race in America in *A Historical Guide to Walt Whitman* (New York: Oxford University Press, 2000); and Ted Genoways for encouraging me to put down in writing my views of Whitman's attitudes toward America and its presidents in the special Whitman issue of the *Virginia Quarterly Review* (Spring 2005).

I thank the Special Collections librarians at the University of Iowa Libraries for their truly remarkable help: Sid Huttner, David Schoonover, and Kathryn Hodson have helped me in so many ways over the years that I cannot begin to catalog their contributions here. The facsimile pages of *Democratic Vistas* in this volume come from a copy owned

by the University of Iowa Libraries, and Gary Frost, conser-
vator, who knows more about books as physical objects than
anyone I have encountered, helped make this facsimile possible. My good friend Ken Reed, one of the great collectors
of Whitman materials, has been amazingly generous over
the years in sharing both the materials he has collected and
the knowledge he has amassed.

Democratic Vistas is at once a distinctly American book
and also a book opening out onto international democratic
issues. I thank my colleagues in the Transatlantic Whitman
Association—including Walter Grünzweig, Wynn Thomas,
Mario Corona, Marina Camboni, Éric Athenot, Maria Clara
Paro, and Marta Skwara—for showing me how vast the
vistas of democracy and democratic friendship are.

The Whitman Series at the University of Iowa Press has
developed in many surprising and delightful ways over the
past decade, and Holly Carver, the director of the Press, has
always been a joy to work with, questioning, suggesting,
probing, and reminding. She has kept the series alive and
kicking.

Work on this book was made possible by a fellowship from
the John Simon Guggenheim Foundation and by a develop-
mental assignment from the College of Arts and Sciences at
the University of Iowa. Finally, I am grateful as always to the
Obermann Center for Advanced Studies at the University of
Iowa and its director, Jay Semel, for generous support over
many years.

{ Abbreviations }

C
Walt Whitman, *The Correspondence*,
ed. Edwin Haviland Miller (New York: New York University
Press, 1961–1977), 6 vols.; vol. 7, ed. Ted Genoways
(Iowa City: University of Iowa Press, 2004).

DBN
Walt Whitman, *Daybooks and Notebooks*, ed. William White
(New York: New York University Press, 1978), 3 vols.

J
Walt Whitman, *The Journalism*, ed. Herbert Bergmann
(New York: Peter Lang, 1998, 2003), 2 vols.

LG
Walt Whitman, *Leaves of Grass: Comprehensive
Reader's Edition*, ed. Harold W. Blodgett and Sculley Bradley
(New York: New York University Press, 1965).

NUPM
Walt Whitman, *Notebooks and Unpublished Prose
Manuscripts*, ed. Edward F. Grier (New York:
New York University Press, 1984), 6 vols.

PW
Walt Whitman, *Prose Works 1892*, ed. Floyd Stovall
(New York: New York University Press, 1963–1964), 2 vols.

WWE
Walt Whitman: An Encyclopedia, ed. J. R. LeMaster and
Donald D. Kummings (New York: Garland, 1998).

WWWC
Horace Traubel, *With Walt Whitman in Camden*
(Various publishers, 1906–1996), 9 vols.

{ Textual Note }

Whitman had originally imagined *Democratic Vistas* would be a text that, like *Leaves of Grass*, would expand and evolve over many years. In a manuscript sketch of himself that he wrote in the third person, Whitman said: "Besides LEAVES OF GRASS this author has also published a prose work, DEMOCRATIC VISTAS, treating of religious, social, political and artistic topics, with immediate reference to the present and the future of the United States. It is said that these VISTAS are purposed to be added to by successive accumulations, in the same way as the poems" (*NUPM* 874).

Those imagined "successive accumulations" never happened, however, and, when Whitman decided to include *Democratic Vistas* in his centennial volume, *Two Rivulets* (1876), he used the same plates that his publisher J. S. Redfield had used for the original 1871 edition. The first edition of *Two Rivulets* was issued in a limited printing of one hundred copies, and it is possible that Whitman simply sewed in unbound sheets of *Vistas* that were left over from the 1871 press run; no changes to the plates were made. When he then decided to issue a larger printing of *Two Rivulets* a few months later, he worked with his friend Harry Bonsall at the printing facilities of the Camden, New Jersey, *Post* and made several small alterations in the *Vistas* plates to correct errors. Joel Myerson in his *Walt Whitman: A Descriptive Bibliography* (Pittsburgh: University of Pittsburgh Press, 1993) lists all but one of the changes: on page 7, line 6 of the footnote, "far-back" is changed to "far back"; on page 14, line 5 of footnote, "woman" is changed to "women"; on page 22, line 25, "got" is changed to "get"; on page 24, line 37, "Spiritual, the aspirational, shall fully" is changed to "Spiritual, shall fully"; on page 36, line 19, "poets" is changed to "Poets"; on page 64, line 31, "is, I" is changed to "is I"; on page 72, line 21, "price"

is changed to "price."; on page 76, line 39, "(of" is changed
to "(the"; and on page 81, line 30, "Cervantes" is changed to
"Cervantes'." A more significant change, not noted by Myerson, is made on page 60, first line following the space break,
where Whitman changes "When the hundredth year of this
Union arrives" to "Long ere the Second Centennial arrives";
this change is discussed in the annotations for page 60, following the essay.

The facsimile text in this volume is reproduced from the
original plates of *Democratic Vistas*, as altered by Whitman
in 1876, so it is the second printing of the original 1871 edition. We have used the second printing because the 1871
printing was poorly inked, and many of the letters in that
version appear broken. Whitman always believed he was
cursed by printers who did not ink his plates properly. He
believed any one of his books "looks better, reads better,
is better, when black-inked—when the ink has not been
spared" (*WWWC* 7:402), and he complained when printers
failed to "ink well" and instead maddeningly used ink "very
sparingly" (*WWWC* 5:89). He had more control over the
1876 printing of the revised plates, and the inking, while not
perfect, was improved. In a manuscript of an unpublished
preface for *Democratic Vistas*, Whitman warned that "I had
better say here at once that he or she who is not willing to
give the book at least two or three perusals, had better leave
it untouched altogether." He was talking about the difficulty
for the reader of absorbing material that he had "combined
together" and that "at first reading may appear incongruous,"
but he may as well also have been talking about the challenge he presented to the reader with his choice of small type
and with the poor quality of the printing (*NUPM* 865). Both
of these qualities were a sign of Whitman's financial plight,
since he was paying for the publication, and it would not be
until he finally printed the essay in his *Specimen Days and
Collect*, with new and much-improved plates, that reading

Democratic Vistas finally became easy on the eyes. By then, though, Whitman had made many changes to this essay, and this facsimile printing of the original edition allows today's readers to once again experience the essay as his readers in the 1870s did.

The Vistas of *Democratic Vistas*

AN INTRODUCTION

ED FOLSOM

Whitman's powerful and evocative title, *Democratic Vistas*, is much better known than the essay it names. Widely used in American culture over the past century, "democratic vistas" has served as the title for numerous books and countless essays and has become a kind of shorthand phrase for that distinctly American sense that the nation's egalitarian fulfillment is always just on the horizon, the faith that our founding ideals are not behind us but always still ahead of us, in our perpetually beckoning future. So, when the *New York Times* wanted a title for its Book Review section focusing on Barack Obama's inauguration, it embraced Whitman's title; "Democratic Vistas" once again seemed to sum up the feelings of the nation after it had elected its first African American president. The cover of the January 18, 2009, issue of the Book Review carried the inscription "Democratic Vistas: Inauguration 2009" over an illustration by Richard McGuire showing Obama, from the back, taking the oath of office as he looked out over Washington, D.C., onto a vista stretching across the continent, with the Golden Gate Bridge in the dim distance.

McGuire's illustration puts us in the position of looking over Obama's shoulder to contemplate the same vast potentiality that the first African American president now gazes on. Like McGuire's image, Whitman's essay evokes the sense that national democratic fulfillment would occur in some unrealized future, speaking differently, *meaning* differently, to succeeding generations of Americans. Therefore, it somehow seemed appropriate, as the nation celebrated the election of a president whom Whitman never could have imagined, to speak once again Whitman's memorable title. McGuire's image is remarkably evocative, in part because Whitman's essay, while very much concerned with the future of democracy in America, is in fact silent about the issue of race. Amid all its prophecies and condemnations of the United States, among the hopes and fears it expresses, the essay manages to evade the question of racial equality, even though Whitman wrote *Democratic Vistas* when the Fourteenth and Fifteenth Amendments to the Constitution, guaranteeing civil rights to freed slaves and suffrage to male African Americans, went into effect. At the very time he was conceiving his essay, Whitman was living in Washington, D.C., where African Americans first exercised their right to vote and where the African American population was increasing dramatically in those years during and after the Civil War.

We will examine the irony and the importance of Whitman's evasion of the subject of race a bit later, but let us begin by examining the ways in which Whitman's essay *is* appropriate for those occasions on which we experience the expansion of America's democratic dream. Whitman always wrote about democracy itself as something that did not yet exist, something that was only now in the process of evolving. Democracy always remained for Whitman an ideal goal, never a realized practice. He saw democracy as an inevitable evolutionary force in human history, and he did all he could to urge the evolution along, but he was under no illusion that a functioning democratic society would come easily or quickly. His efforts in *Leaves of Grass* had been to try to invent a poetry as open, as nondiscriminatory, and as absorptive as he imagined an ideal democracy would be. He tried, in other words, to construct a democratic voice that would serve as a model for his society—a difficult task since he was well aware that his nation and his world were still filled with antidemocratic sentiments, laws, customs, and institutions, and he knew that no writer, including himself, could rise above all the biases and blindnesses of his particular historical moment. But he was convinced that the United States in the nineteenth century was in the process of becoming the first culture in human history to experience the beginnings of a true democracy.[1]

In the dictionary Whitman used, Webster's *American Dictionary of the English Language*, democracy is defined as "a form of government, in which the supreme power is lodged in the hands of the people collectively, or in which the people exercise the powers of legislation," and the definition ends with a single example: "Such was the government of Athens." This dictionary makes no mention of American democracy. Whitman took issue with this definition, and, when he talks about the evolution of democracy in *Democratic Vistas*, he ignores Athenian democracy. For him, human history is not so much a back-and-forth struggle between democratic and antidemocratic forces as it is an unbroken evolution away from feudalism toward the natural and rational democratic future. When he defines democracy, then, his definition contains no past examples or models, but instead looks only toward the future, which of course renders any act of actual definition impossible. So in *Democratic Vistas*, he offers perhaps the best nondefinition of democracy ever formulated: "We have frequently printed the word Democracy," he says, "yet I cannot too often repeat that it is a word the real gist of which still sleeps, quite unawaken'd." He goes on to say that it is a "great word, whose history, I suppose, remains unwritten, because that history has yet to be enacted." Democracy, in other words, is the most significant word in the American language and yet remains a word for which there is still no definition, because no society has yet lived the history that would illustrate it. Again and again in *Democratic Vistas*, this idea emerges: Whitman assumes

"Democracy to be at present in its embryo condition," and he insists that "the fruition of democracy . . . resides altogether in the future."

Whitman also disagreed with Webster's emphasis on the "form of government" as the essential aspect of a democracy. What is most striking about Whitman's emphasis in *Democratic Vistas* is his insistence that a democratic *literature* was the most essential factor, for as long as the imagination of the country remained shackled by feudalistic models of literature, by romances that reinforced power hierarchies and gender discrimination, and by a conception of literary production that put authorship only in the hands of the educated elite, then democracy would never flourish, regardless of the form of government. Whitman was finally more intrigued with the way a democratic self would act than the way a democratic society would function, and the defining of this revolutionary new self, he knew, was a job for the poet. A democracy, then, would require a new kind of imaginative relationship between reader and author, a more equalizing give and take, and so Whitman argued that "a new Literature," a "democratic literature of the future," and especially "a new Poetry, are to be, in my opinion, the only sure and worthy supports and expressions of the American democracy." The greatest duty of the American poet, Whitman believed, was to write the "epic of democracy," to go about the business of "making a new history, a history of democracy, making the old history a dwarf" (*PW* 2:522). The poet of democracy would change a nation's reading habits and in so doing would create the imaginative energy necessary to break down feudalistic assumptions and to construct a new democratic frame of mind. That is why, in *Democratic Vistas*, Whitman emphasizes not just the need for a new democratic literature, but for a muscular, rebellious, democratic *reader*, capable of engaging, challenging, and *completing* the demands of the new literature: "Books are to be call'd for, and supplied, on the assumption that the process of reading is not a half-sleep, but, in highest sense, an exercise, a gymnast's struggle; that the reader is to do something for himself, must be on the alert, must himself or herself construct indeed the poem, argument, history, metaphysical essay—the text furnishing the hints, the clue, the start or frame-work. Not the book needs so much to be the complete thing, but the reader of the book does. That were to make a nation of supple and athletic minds, well-train'd, intuitive, used to depend on themselves, and not on a few coteries of writers."

Whitman was not a naive apologist for democracy. He regularly cast a skeptical eye on American culture, and, as he makes clear at the beginning of *Democratic Vistas*, he was keenly aware of the many shortcomings of the then-current state of American democracy as well as of some of the basic contradictions of democratic theory. It would be hard to find a more bracing critique of the state of America than the one Whitman offers near the beginning of the essay as he takes on the role of a physician examining the diseased body politic of the nation: "I say we had best look our times and lands searchingly in the face, like a physician diagnosing some deep disease. Never was there, perhaps, more hollowness at heart than at present, and here in the United States. . . . The spectacle is appalling. We live in an atmosphere of hypocrisy throughout." As always, though, Whitman tried to view the appalling present as a stage America had to go through to achieve its promising future. During the Civil War, for example, Whitman castigated the U.S. military for its feudalistic and antidemocratic organization, and yet he also argued that two of the great "proofs" of democracy in America were the voluntary arming of the troops and the peaceful disbanding of the armies after the war was over (*PW* 1:25). The military thus at once offered distressing and hopeful signs, as it, like much of American society, struggled (as it continues to do today) to discover the implications of democratic reformation.

Still, by the time he wrote *Democratic Vistas*, Whitman was less sanguine than he had ever been about democracy's inevitable success. He begins his essay by alternately agreeing with and disputing the Scottish essayist Thomas Carlyle's famous attacks on democracy. As Whitman gradually builds a case for the continuing evolution of American democracy and the need for a more spiritual phase of democracy to replace the material phase that the country seemed mired in after the Civil War, he wrestles with the thorny problems of democratic theory, especially the irresolvable tension between the many and the one, between the social cohesion necessary to make a democracy work and the equally important necessity of individual freedom. For Whitman, the issue was always the negotiation of the "democratic individual" with "democratic nationality" (*PW* 2:463). In the essay, he names his provisional solution to this problem "Personalism," a blending of the one and the many, a balancing of individuality with camaraderie—the love for one's democratic and equal others in all their diversity balanced against the pride in one's own identity. In order to "counterbalance and offset" the "materialistic and vulgar American democracy," Whitman looked to "the development, identification, and general prevalence of that fervid comradeship, (the adhesive love, at least rivaling the amative love)."

For Whitman, then, a democratic self was one that came to recognize vast multitudes of possibility within its own identity, one that could imagine how one's own identity, given altered circumstances, might incorporate the identity of anyone in the culture, from the most marginalized to the most exalted and powerful. To experience democratic selfhood, then, an American needed to engage in the radical act of imagining how she or he could share an identity with every member of the society, of learning to love difference by recognizing the possibility of that difference within a multitudinous self, a self that had been enlarged by non-discriminatory practice, nurtured by a new absorptive and antifeudalistic literature, and enriched by love that crossed conventional boundaries. *Democratic Vistas* stands as Whitman's most eloquent and extended articulation of the hazy, beckoning, illusive American democratic future.

Whitman's genius in *Democratic Vistas* may in fact have resided in his ability to focus on the nation's future vistas instead of on its degraded present. Had Whitman simply engaged the problems America was facing in the late 1860s about reuniting the nation and granting civil rights to freed slaves, his essay might well have ended up being an interesting historical piece but not the enduring cultural document it has become. Still, it is important to place this essay at the scene of its writing, to know just where Whitman was when he wrote the essay, just what he was doing, just what social and political environment he found himself in, and just what he was thinking about the major issues of the day, for all of these elements were vital aspects of the construction of *Democratic Vistas*. This was an essay conceived and written in Washington, D.C., and it is Whitman's quintessential Washington publication, growing out of his interactions with the tens of thousands of Civil War soldiers he cared for in D.C. hospitals, out of his experience as a government clerk, where he directly engaged most of the major social and political issues that confronted America during and after the war, and out of his daily life as a citizen of the nation's capital, a city on the edge of the South whose populace was not happy with what the war had brought to town. It is no accident that Whitman chose to put "Washington, D.C., 1871" prominently on both the cover and title page of his book, for this was a work that grew organically out of its time and place every bit as much as the original *Leaves of*

Grass grew out of Brooklyn, New York, in 1855 (as *its* title page clearly announced).

When we picture Whitman in Washington, D.C., we tend to imagine him during the Civil War, as he observed Abraham Lincoln when the president rode back and forth from the White House to his summer retreat at the Soldiers' Home, journeys occasionally marked by the president and the poet nodding to each other as Lincoln passed by; visiting the wounded soldiers in the many makeshift hospitals that dotted the capital during the war; being fired from his clerk's position in the Department of the Interior by Secretary James Harlan, who disapproved of the poet's immoral writings and perhaps also of his habit of working on his poetry during job hours (and then, just after the war, being defended so eloquently by his friend William Douglas O'Connor, who published his scathing attack on Harlan and his hagiographic exoneration of Whitman in his 1866 pamphlet *The Good Gray Poet*). But in many ways the most revealing part of Whitman's residency in Washington occurred in the five years following the war, as Whitman found himself at the very center of the nation's massive attempt to reconstruct and redefine itself. This politically chaotic era was the period that produced *Democratic Vistas*.

While entire books have been written on the Whitman/ Lincoln associations, and everyone knows Whitman's elegies for the assassinated president, "O Captain! My Captain!" and "When Lilacs Last in the Dooryard Bloom'd," very little has been written on the much closer relationship Whitman had with Lincoln's vice president and successor, Andrew Johnson from Tennessee. While Whitman wrote no poems about Johnson, he generally endorsed the beleaguered president's policies and emulated his attitude of forgiveness toward the South. Whitman worked for all three of Johnson's attorneys general during the four years Johnson served out Lincoln's second term (1865–1869). These were quieter years in Whitman's personal life, but the scene around him was tumultuous as Congress, led by radical Republicans, set out to construct a multiracial society, and as President Johnson tried to resist, developing an enmity with Congress that would lead to his impeachment. The tumultuous year of 1865—which saw the surrender of the Confederacy, the assassination of Lincoln and attempted assassination of Secretary of State William Seward, the killing of Lincoln's assassin John Wilkes Booth and the trial and conviction of his co-conspirators, the capturing of the Confederacy's president Jefferson Davis, President Johnson's attempts to restore the Union largely by forgiving those states that rebelled and turning their governance over to Southerners, and the growing hostility between Congress and Johnson— ended with the ratification of the Thirteenth Amendment to the Constitution, abolishing slavery throughout the United States and its territories, and thus completing and making permanent Lincoln's Emancipation Proclamation.

But the real challenges were just beginning. Over four million freed slaves were now on their own in America, existing in some halfway state between slavery and citizenship, emancipated but without civil rights and anything but integrated into American society. Before the war, many white leaders in government and elsewhere—including Lincoln and Harriet Beecher Stowe (whose *Uncle Tom's Cabin* had become an antislavery sensation)—had called for the removal of freed slaves to Africa or to the Caribbean or elsewhere, where they could develop their own culture and not disturb the nation's status quo. But the war had changed everything, and the hopes of many whites that an orderly removal of former slaves from the continent could be carried out vanished when Lincoln issued the Emancipation Proclamation at the beginning of 1863 and invited the newly freed slaves to enlist in the Union army. When General William Tecumseh Sherman's Union march through Georgia cut

Price, 75 Cents.

Democratic

VISTAS.

Washington, D. C.

1871.

NEW-YORK: J. S. REDFIELD, PUBLISHER, 140 Fulton St., (up stairs.)

Front cover of the 1870–71 *Democratic Vistas*.

Back cover of the 1870–71 *Democratic Vistas.*

a path of destruction to the Atlantic Ocean, his all-white troops encountered an unexpected problem: the slaves who were released from the plantations had nowhere to go and so began to follow the Northern troops, who for the most part wanted nothing to do with these newly freed people and tried everything they could to separate them from the army. Before emancipation, Union forces had set up contraband camps in various locations during the war to hold the human "property" of the South, and some of these camps continued to exist after emancipation, forming into working communities of former slaves and becoming some of the first African American towns in the United States.

Washington, D.C., quickly became the site of America's first experiments in a multiracial society. The Compensated Emancipation Act, which went into effect on April 16, 1862, freed slaves in the capital city, nearly nine months before Lincoln announced his more general Emancipation Proclamation. Slaveholders in D.C. were paid for their emancipated slaves, the only widespread compensated emancipation program ever undertaken in the country. As the first emancipated city, Washington attracted many freed and runaway slaves from that point on. As the Fourteenth and Fifteenth Amendments to the Constitution were passed, establishing civil rights for blacks, including the right of black men to vote, thousands of additional former slaves came to Washington, where, they were convinced, they stood the best chance of having those new rights protected. The black population of D.C. grew from 18 percent in 1860 to 33 percent in 1870. And Congress was determined to make D.C. a showcase for racial equality, even if Washington's white citizens were vehemently opposed.

Near the end of 1865, Congress had decided to go a step further with their social experiment in Washington by granting African Americans in D.C. the right to vote, nearly five years before the Fifteenth Amendment would extend that right across the nation. An outraged Washington Board of Aldermen responded by passing a resolution demanding that the mayor hold a special election "to ascertain the opinion of the people of Washington on the question of Negro Suffrage." The referendum was held on December 21, 1865, and the results were stunning: 6,591 voted against Negro suffrage, and only thirty-five for it. Voters came out for this special election in droves: the vote total for the referendum was in fact larger than for the mayoral elections in 1862 and 1864. Richard Wallach, the mayor, reported the results to the U.S. Senate, pointedly noting that the only people (in addition to the thirty-five citizens voting yes) who supported the black vote were Washington's temporary residents—the Congressmen themselves—who maintained their franchise elsewhere and had "no community of interest or affinity with the citizens of Washington." A similar referendum was held in Georgetown on December 28, with a similar result: 712 against, only one in favor. Congress nonetheless pushed forward with the plan, aware that the influx of blacks into the city from Maryland and Virginia had the potential to give the Republicans control of the city government, since the new black voters could be counted on to vote with the radical Republicans who were working for civil rights for the freed slaves. In early January 1866, Congress passed a new voting statute for D.C., giving all males over the age of twenty-one who were not "infamous" criminals or Southern sympathizers the right to vote, without regard to race, property, and educational training (thus granting the former slaves the right to vote while withholding that right from the former slave owners).[2] Whitman is silent in his correspondence and in his journalism about these momentous events, but he discussed them vigorously with W. D. O'Connor, Charles Eldridge, John Trowbridge, and the others who gathered in the O'Connor home nightly to debate the issues of the day.

While attending the Congressional debates that were

deciding to what extent blacks would be allowed entry into the reconstructed nation, Whitman looked at the changed world about him: "We had the greatest black procession here last Thursday—I didn't think there was so many dark-eys, (especially wenches,) in the world—it was the anniversary of emancipation in this District" (*C* 1:273–274). The tone of this April 1866 letter to his mother is tricky to read: Whitman had just experienced the first Emancipation Day celebration, which would take place annually in Washington every April throughout the rest of the century (again, Lincoln signed the Compensated Emancipation Act, freeing enslaved people in the District of Columbia, on April 16, 1862), and Whitman sees the procession as "great," but his description of the new black citizens as countless "darkeys" and "wenches" suggests that he was at this time closer to the views of the vast majority of white citizens in D.C. than we might like to think.

The first election African Americans voted in was held in June of 1867, for some aldermen and assorted minor offices. Candidates that blacks supported did very well, because many whites boycotted that election. Having learned their lesson, whites turned out for the mayoral election in June of 1868, as did Washington's growing black population, a population inflated, many Democrats charged, by the illegal importation of freed slaves from surrounding states, just in time to meet the reduced fifteen-day precinct residency requirement enacted at the last minute by the Republicans. Nearly eight thousand blacks were registered to vote, and twelve thousand whites. Over eighteen thousand total voters showed up at the polls and elected Sayles Jenks Bowen (1813–1896), one of the most controversial mayors in Washington's history. A radical Republican who fought bravely and tirelessly for black civil rights, he carried virtually all of the black votes, and he eked out a razor-thin victory over his Democratic opponent, John T. Given, who contested the results. Bowen had 9,170 votes to Given's 9,087; assuming that Bowen received nearly eight thousand black votes, he would then have had the support of only one in ten white voters. (Fortunately for Bowen, given the volatile situation, he had been police commissioner of the city, and his connections to the police department served him well when he had to break down the doors of the mayor's office with police support in order to take physical possession of the city offices.) Bowen embarked on an aggressive reformist agenda, setting out to fully integrate D.C. public schools, and, when he was unable to accomplish that, working tirelessly (and contributing substantial sums of his own money) to develop a network of schools for blacks. He appointed African Americans to high administrative posts, and during his term blacks were elected to the city council. After the city's debt increased dramatically, he failed in his re-election bid in 1870.[3]

Whitman's one comment on Bowen's election came in a June 1868 letter, written just after the election took place. African Americans were taking to Washington's streets more and more frequently, and Whitman responded with disdain and a growing alarm; he wrote again to his mother:

> We had the strangest procession here last Tuesday night, about 3000 darkeys, old & young, men & women—I saw them all—they turned out in honor of *their* victory in electing the Mayor, Mr. Bowen—the men were all armed with clubs or pistols—besides the procession in the street, there was a string went along the sidewalk in single file with bludgeons & sticks, yelling & gesticulating like madmen—it was quite comical, yet very disgusting & alarming in some respects—They were very insolent, & altogether it was a strange sight—they looked like so many wild brutes let loose—thousands of slaves from the Southern plantations have crowded up here— many are supported by the Gov't. (*C* 2:34–35)

Just three years earlier, Whitman had described with real admiration the black troops marching in Lincoln's second inauguration parade, "in full uniform, with guns on their shoulders," heading to the nurturing breast of the Capitol with its newly completed "milky bulging dome," raising their faces toward "the star of the West," becoming "well worth looking at themselves, as new styles of physiognomical pictures."[4] Now these handsome and orderly troops had transmuted into a swarm of madmen with clubs, pistols, bludgeons, and sticks. What had been, two years earlier, "the greatest black procession" now had become "the strangest procession." Whitman clearly was beginning to doubt the promise of a racially integrated nation.[5] His comment about how Bowen's election was "*their* victory" underscores his belief that a major problem with black suffrage was that blacks would vote only in a block and would not think as individuals about issues and candidates. Twenty years later he was still concerned about this tendency, noting that he agreed with the Southern journalist Henry Watterson's view "that the Negro franchise would never be truly granted till the Negro vote was a divided, not a class one." "I know enough of Southern affairs," Whitman told Horace Traubel, "have associated enough with Southern people to feel convinced that if I lived South I should side with the Southern whites." Traubel was alarmed and asked Whitman how such a view meshed with his ideas about democracy. "I should be forced not to explain that," Whitman answered; "I would have to evade the issue" (*WWWC* 7:158).

It was during the two years of Bowen's administration that Whitman wrote *Democratic Vistas*, a project he initially conceived of as a response to Thomas Carlyle's racist diatribe in his 1867 essay, "Shooting Niagara—and After?" Whitman set out to address the burning issue in America of black suffrage, but by the time the essay was published, just after Bowen had been soundly defeated in his bid for re-election, African Americans were absent, and the issue of suffrage was reduced to a whisper in an after-note, where race was perhaps implied but not explicitly mentioned ("As to general suffrage, after all, since we have gone so far, the more general it is, the better. I favor the widest opening of the doors. Let the ventilation and area be wide enough, and all is safe").[6] And then, when he reprinted *Democratic Vistas*, he removed even that note and buried it deep in his "Notes Left Over" section of *Collect*.[7] The only notes on his encounters with black troops that make it into his collected writings did not get published until he included some old fragments in *November Boughs* in 1888.[8] Erasing race from his work during the final twenty-five years of his life was one of Whitman's occupations, as he became increasingly silent about one of the defining issues of American history. He left behind, however, enough traces that we can still glimpse the beginnings of his once brave vision, his attempt to imagine a democratic subjectivity open enough to speak black experience in often subtle ways, a vision that began with his first notes toward *Leaves of Grass* but lasted only until soon after the Civil War ended, when the real work of building a multiracial society was just getting underway. After freed slaves were allowed to enlist in the Union Army in 1863, Whitman carefully cut out and kept newspaper articles about black troops and noted their bravery and prowess; these clippings suggest that he had a major project in mind, writing about how the liberated slaves were quickly becoming absorbed into America, their emerging equality forged in the crucible of battle. But the project never materialized.

Whitman at the time was a government clerk, and this is how he was listed in the D.C. directory, not as a poet but as one of the countless bureaucrats who held such jobs (government officials were the third most common job in D.C. at the time, after servants and laborers). When he wrote his meditation on democracy's future, then, he did so from the

perspective of someone buried deep in the government bureaucracy, working for the attorney general, tediously copy-
ing the documents that kept the government running. But it
is important to recall that government bureaucracy was still
in its infancy at this point. It was only in the 1850s that the
attorney general became a full-time position. Caleb Cushing,
serving as attorney general under President Franklin Pierce,
successfully argued for the position having equal responsi-
bilities and stature to the secretary of state and secretary of
the treasury; he also centralized in his office legal respon-
sibilities that had been scattered to other departments like
Interior and State. The attorney general did not even have
an assistant until 1859. But the office grew as it became the
center of controversy during the Civil War, when Attorney
General Edward Bates had to defend and justify Lincoln's
use of emergency war powers, including his suspension of
habeas corpus, and had to tread the fine legal line between
defining the Civil War as a war or an insurrection. Then,
when James Speed became attorney general in 1864, the
office was embroiled in the controversy over whether or not
military courts had jurisdiction over civilian populations.[9]
When Whitman joined the attorney general's staff in the
summer of 1865, then, he was placing himself in one of the
most volatile centers of American political life, as the attorney general's office became the enforcement agency for the
new civil rights amendments to the Constitution, outlawing
slavery and granting equal protection and suffrage to the
freed slaves. The prosecution of cases against the Ku Klux
Klan—the South's ugly vigilante answer to the new amendments and to newly passed civil rights legislation—was directed from the office in which Whitman worked. During
the years he worked there, the office was overwhelmed with
work and lacked the resources to handle the cases it was
called on to prosecute.[10]

Whitman was among the first generation of clerks hired

in the attorney general's office. In 1859, just before the Civil War, the attorney general's office consisted of the attorney general, the assistant attorney general, and three clerks; its annual appropriation (including salaries) was $17,500.[11] While Whitman was working there, the office grew, as after the war it became a central player in all the legal tangles brought on by Reconstruction, including issuing thousands of pardons for former Confederates. But by 1868, the office had an annual appropriation of only $63,590,[12] and the number of personnel was still small. The attorney general's office was tucked into the southwest corner of the Treasury Building and consisted of just a few rooms. Even when the Department of Justice was formed in 1870, the number of employees totaled sixteen, including only six full-time clerks.[13] Whitman worked closely and directly with the seven attorneys general under whom he served until 1872, and he came to know them and their assistant attorneys general quite well. Most of the time that he worked for the attorney general, he was in an office of under a dozen workers, whose boss knew them all. Just as he had done for countless soldiers in the hospitals, he wrote letters every day for others, signing their names instead of his, filtering their news through his own mind and hand. And, as with the Civil War soldiers' experiences, the matters he wrote about worked their way into his poetry and prose. He wrote about pardons for Southerners, civil rights for freed slaves, and the reunification of the states. It was a troubled time, but as he copied the legal documents that worked to bind the country back together, his mind, while continually aware of the challenges that faced America, nonetheless wandered to the nation's democratic vistas.

By 1871, Whitman would have been all too familiar with the experience of constructing his books to be widely read in his own country, only to have them sell poorly. He always had inflated hopes for the success of every book he published. He confidently concluded his preface to the first edition of *Leaves of Grass* (1855) by claiming that "the proof of a poet is that his country absorbs him as affectionately as he has absorbed it" (*LG* 729). But "affection" was hardly the appropriate term for the mostly vituperative reviews the first edition of *Leaves* received, and absorption by his country seemed faintly ridiculous after only a couple of dozen of the 795 copies he printed were sold. The next year, when he issued his second edition, he bravely predicted that in "a few years" "the average annual call for my Poems is ten or twenty thousand copies—more, quite likely" (*LG* 731). A thousand copies of the second edition were printed, but sales were again disappointing, and Whitman would never experience annual sales even approaching ten or twenty thousand copies. Nevertheless, he remained convinced that somehow he was indeed speaking for and to the nation, and so he gradually began casting his faith in future readers and adjusting his poems to speak to audiences "a generation, or ever so many generations hence" (*LG* 160), aware that the affection and absorption he dreamed of needed to be deferred until the country was ready for him. As America's evolving democracy gradually developed a democratic readership, Whitman believed, so would the nation eventually develop an appetite for his work. But he nonetheless always hoped against hope that something he would publish in his own lifetime would catch fire with his contemporary readers.

So when, in the years immediately following the Civil War, he began making notes toward a series of prose essays that would assess the future of the United States as it gathered and tried to rejoin the shattered pieces of the country, he once again had high hopes that his analysis of American democracy would have an immediate and widespread impact. Setting out to answer in various ways Matthew Arnold and Thomas Carlyle, who towered over Britain as the most prominent public intellectuals of their day, and engaging as well Ralph Waldo Emerson, whose prose essays in America had the same stature as Arnold's and Carlyle's did in England, Whitman sought now to intervene in the major social issues of his time, but this time to do so in prose instead of poetry. Britain had a long tradition of distinguished prose essayists, who wrote powerful and far-reaching critiques of the current state of British society, guiding the reading public through the cultural tumult of the nineteenth century, with all its confusing and discomfiting encounters with the implications of Charles Darwin's evolutionary theories that challenged the notion that man was created in the image of God, Charles Lyell's geological discoveries that extended the very scope of time that allowed the slow workings of evolution to become conceivable, astronomical discoveries that were expanding the size and increasing the age of the universe beyond imagining, political revolutions that were upsetting the history of how societies were organized and governed, historical criticism of the Bible that—combined with the findings in science—seemed to be shattering the very foundations of traditional religious faith. In such an environment, as Terry Eagleton has noted, "the man of letters found himself a consoler as well as a critic, increasingly adopting a soothing bedside manner to quell the anxieties of the middle classes."[14]

Throughout Whitman's lifetime, a remarkable number of British essayists—from Carlyle and Arnold through Thomas Babington Macaulay, John Henry Newman, John Stuart Mill, John Ruskin, Thomas Henry Huxley, William Morris, Walter Pater, and many others—addressed every imaginable social, artistic, philosophical, scientific, and religious topic. These essayists still form a major part of the Victorian literature that is studied today. But if we look for a comparable tradition in the United States, we come up with a surprisingly slim list. Emerson towered over other American essayists and certainly is the equal of any of the British Victorians, though his essays tended to address universal issues instead of contemporary social problems. Beyond Emerson, though, it seems that America simply did not produce such figures. Henry David Thoreau, had he lived through the century, might have developed into such a writer, and certainly others—like Mark Twain, William Dean Howells, and Henry James—wrote important essays on a variety of social, political, and aesthetic issues, though their prowess in fiction dwarfs their achievements in the essay form, unlike many of the Victorians, for whom the essay was their signature achievement. And the work of the true social essayists in nineteenth-century America, like Thomas Wentworth Higginson, has been largely neglected in our literary histories.

With *Democratic Vistas*, then, Whitman set out to write an essay that would put him in the company of the great British prose writers of the century. Trained as a printer and with long experience as a newspaper writer and editor, Whitman was of course no stranger to prose. Beyond his journalistic pieces, many of which dealt with the political and social issues of the day, he wrote some early and extended prose essays—like "Slavery—the Slaveholders" and "The Eighteenth Presidency!" in the 1850s—that were never published but which indicate that his desire to be a controversial social essayist was longstanding. During the Civil War, he published prose essays and reports about the war in the *New York Times* and many other prominent papers. All of these writings were pointing toward *Memoranda During the War*, his prose book about the war, his experiences in Washington, D.C., during the war, and his intensive work in the Civil War hospitals that dotted the Union capital city. Typically, he had convinced himself that his Civil War prose book could be a best-seller, could maybe be marketed to the soldiers themselves, who, he believed, would recognize in his writing a kind of intimate knowledge of themselves. He proposed his "new book" to the radical author and publisher James Redpath in 1863, pointedly claiming that his memoranda would be much different from and better than Louisa May Alcott's best-selling *Hospital Sketches*; his work, he claimed, would be "a book of the time, worthy the time—something considerably beyond mere hospital sketches" (*C* 1:171). Redpath, however, fended Whitman off, citing financial worries, and, by the time the war ended, Whitman's book still had not appeared. It would not appear until over a decade later, when he brought it out with his own money, still forced into the self-publishing he had become so accustomed to.

Meanwhile, he was working on his new series of prose essays defining American democracy, essays that he hoped would position him to become a dominant social critic. He decided to take on two of the most powerful British essayists, Carlyle and Arnold, who continued to sow doubt about America's democratic experiment and who were cautioning America, especially in the chaotic years after the Civil War, not to go too far, not to (as Carlyle put it) "shoot Niagara" and risk ruin by giving in to mobocracy or (to use Carlyle's term) "Swarmery," but instead to preserve (as Arnold would have it) culture over anarchy. In August, Whitman read Carlyle's "Shooting Niagara: and After?" Carlyle's piece had appeared in England in *Macmillan's* in August of 1867 and was quickly reprinted in the United States; Whitman read it in the New York *Tribune*, when Horace Greeley reprinted it on August 16. It was widely reprinted, and it seems that everyone was discussing it. Whitman had long been a fan of Carlyle's writing, reviewing it regularly in the *Brooklyn Daily Eagle* in the mid-1840s. He noted how in *Heroes and Hero Worship*, "under his rapt, wierd [*sic*], (grotesque?) style," Carlyle "has placed—we may almost say *hidden*—many noble thoughts," and he surprisingly described Carlyle, a skeptic about democracy, as "a Democrat in that enlarged sense which we would fain see more men Democrats;—that he is quick to champion the downtrodden, and earnest in his wrath at tyranny."[15] *Sartor Resartus*, Whitman said, "has all of Mr. Carlyle's strange wild way;—and all his fiery-breath and profundity of meaning—when you delve them out" (*J* 2:105). He briefly reviewed *The French Revolution*, and in his review of *Past and Present* and *Chartism*, he once again noted Carlyle's "wierd, wild way—his phrases, welded together as it were, with strange twistings of the terminatives of words—his startling suggestions—his taking up, fish-hook like, certain matters of abuse—make an *original* kind of composition, that gets after a little usage, to be strangely agreeable!" "One likes Mr. Carlyle," Whitman said, "the more he communes with him" (*J* 2:131, 244).

It is as if Whitman at this point was discovering in Carlyle the kind of license for stylistic freedom and idiosyncrasy that, a few years later, he would discover for himself as he composed *Leaves of Grass*. Critics have traced many echoes of Carlyle's work in *Leaves*, and it is clear that in the years when Whitman was writing his first book of poetry, Carlyle was one of the authors he was most frequently reading. He owned all of Carlyle's books, held on to them, and returned to them frequently.[16] He continued to love what he called in an 1858 review of Carlyle's *History of Frederick the Great* "his startling outbursts of eloquence couched in language as startling."[17] At the time of Carlyle's death in 1881, Whitman praised Carlyle for "launching into the self-complacent atmosphere of our days a rasping, questioning, dislocating agitation and shock" (*PW* 1:250). During his last years, Whitman compared Carlyle to President Andrew Jackson: "Jackson had something of Carlyle in him: a touch of irascibility: quarrelsome, testy, threatening humors: still was always finally honest, like Carlyle." Agreeing or disagreeing with Carlyle was never the point for Whitman; what was important was that, as he put it, "Carlyle always stirs me to the deeps."[18] For Whitman, Carlyle's "final value" was the way he launched "into the self-complacent atmosphere of our days a rasping, questioning, dislocating agitation and shock" (*PW* 1:250). All these qualities were apparent in one of Carlyle's most rasping, quarrelsome, agitating, shocking, and threatening essays, "Shooting Niagara," and it stirred Whitman to respond immediately.

"Shooting Niagara: and After?" is mostly about Carlyle's anxiety over changes in British society brought on by the expansion of voting rights and his horror over the thought that "England would have to take the Niagara leap of completed Democracy one day," "towards the Bottomless or into it," with the "Count of Heads to be the Divine Court of Appeal on every question and interest to mankind," so that Britain's "hundred and fifty millions" would be "'free' more and more to follow each his own nose, by way of guide-post in this intricate world."[19] But what caught Whitman's attention and the attention of countless readers in America was Carlyle's vituperative evocation of the United States as the country that was leading the way over the falls to utter destruction, and it was doing so first by freeing its slaves and then by giving them civil rights and the right to vote. His harangue against democracy was most viciously directed toward the multiracial experiment that America had newly embarked on, what Carlyle liked to call "the Nigger Question." Democracy was becoming for him indistinguishable from mob rule, mindless swarms of people blindly following each other, and none were more blind than the newly freed slaves. Carlyle stated his case with a memorable mixture of bombast and casual racism. Here is the passage that prompted Whitman to respond:

> By far the notablest result of *Swarmery*, in these times, is that of the late American War, with Settlement of the Nigger Question for result. Essentially the Nigger Ques-

tion was one of the smallest; and in itself did not much
concern mankind in the present time of struggles and
hurries. One always rather likes the Nigger; evidently
a poor blockhead with good dispositions, with affec-
tions, attachments,—with a turn for Nigger Melodies,
and the like:—he is the only Savage of all the coloured
races that doesn't die out on sight of the White Man;
but can actually live beside him, and work and increase
and be merry. The Almighty Maker has appointed him
to be a Servant. . . . Servantship, like all solid contracts
between men (like wedlock itself, which was *once*
nomadic enough, temporary enough!), must become a
contract of permanency, not easy to dissolve, but difficult extremely,—a "contract for life," if you can manage
it (which you cannot, without many wise laws and regulations, and a great deal of earnest thought and anxious
experience), will evidently be the best of all. And this
was already the Nigger's essential position. Mischief,
irregularities, injustices, did probably abound between
Nigger and Buckra [a term Africans used for "white
man"]; but the poisonous taproot of all mischief, and
impossibility of fairness, humanity, or well-doing in the
contract, never had been there! Of all else the remedy
was easy in comparison; vitally important to every just
man concerned in it; and, under all obstructions (which
in the American case, begirt with frantic "Abolitionists,"
fire-breathing like the old Chimæra, were immense),
was gradually getting itself done. To me individually the
Nigger's case was not the most pressing in the world,
but among the least so! America, however, had got into
Swarmery upon it (not America's blame either, but in
great part ours, and that of the nonsense *we* sent over to
them); and felt that in the Heavens or the Earth there
was nothing so godlike, or incomparably pressing to
be done. Their energy, their valour, their &c. &c. were

worthy of the stock they sprang from:—and now, poor
fellows, *done* it is, with a witness. A continent of the
earth has been submerged, for certain years, by deluges
as from the Pit of Hell; half a million (some say a whole
million, but surely they exaggerate) of excellent White
Men, full of gifts and faculty, have slit one another into
horrid death, in a temporary humour, which will leave
centuries of remembrance fierce enough: and three million Blacks, men and brothers (of a sort), are completely
"emancipated;" launched into the career of improvement, — likely to be "improved off the face of the earth"
in a generation or two! (321–322)

It is difficult to imagine just how Whitman must have re-
acted to Carlyle's attack on America, his charge of national
stupidity, his claim that the Civil War and all its carnage was
a useless and self-destructive attempt to undo the proud tradition of "servantship" that African Americans were, so he
claims, made for. Here it was in its starkest form: Lincoln's
grand ideal of emancipation as the fruition of democracy,
reduced to a costly and silly scheme to free and thus to destroy an inferior race. This, pronounces Carlyle, was what
America fought its Civil War for—not worthy ideals, but
blind stupidity. No wonder, we might think, that Whitman
was, as he says in a footnote to *Democratic Vistas*, "roused
to much anger and abuse by this essay from Mr. Carlyle, so
insulting to the theory of America."

Whitman would have bristled at the idea that the Civil
War was a foolhardy exercise of killing hundreds of thousands of "excellent White Men" in order to free "three million absurd Blacks." For Whitman, the war was fought for
the vital goal to preserve the Union, and, while the first three
editions of *Leaves of Grass* portrayed slaves sympathetically
and showed empathetic concern for African Americans,
he in fact had little to say about emancipated slaves or the

Emancipation Proclamation itself. His one recorded comment on the Emancipation Proclamation is a manuscript note that appears to be the beginning of an intended newspaper piece; in it, he calls "the president's proclamation" "a marked and first-class event" that nonetheless failed to produce much excitement in the nation's capital; Whitman notes "the phlegmatic coolness all through Washington, under the new emancipation document." What is most striking to Whitman is that he hears "little allusion made to it in the public places of the city" (*NUPM* 2:545). Whitman is complicit in this cool silence: the issues of slavery and emancipation never enter Whitman's Civil War poems, *Drum-Taps*, nor are they mentioned in his *Memoranda During the War*. The Civil War was a vital, defining event for Whitman, but there is little evidence in his writing during or after the war that he considered race or slavery a key element in the war's importance.

And so, as Whitman began his own diagnosis of "the theory of America," he seemed at first to be ready to tackle the very problem so baldly stated by Carlyle. Again and again in the opening pages of *Democratic Vistas*, Whitman edges toward a confrontation with the issue of interracial democracy, of black suffrage, as he talks of "the priceless value of our political institutions, general suffrage, (and cheerfully acknowledging the latest, widest opening of the doors)," and as he talks of how "so many voices, pens, minds, in the press, lecture-rooms, in our Congress, &c., are discussing intellectual topics, pecuniary dangers, legislative problems, the suffrage." "I will not gloss over the appalling dangers of universal suffrage in the United States," he vows. And in his original *Galaxy* essay that formed the first one-third of *Democratic Vistas*, Whitman did go on to directly engage Carlyle, using an uncharacteristic and uneasy sarcastic tone:

. . . how shall we, good-class folk, meet the rolling, mountainous surges of "swarmery" that already beat upon and threaten to overwhelm us? What disposal, short of wholesale throat-cutting and extermination (which seems not without its advantages), offers, for the countless herds of "hoofs and hobnails," that will some-how, and so perversely get themselves born, and grow up to annoy and vex us? What under heaven is to be-come of "nigger Cushee," that imbruted and lazy being— now, worst of all, preposterously free? . . . Ring the ala-rum bell! Put the flags at the half mast! Or, rather, let each man spring for the nearest loose spar or plank. The ship is going down! (*PW* 2:749)

It is hard to tell how much Whitman's strained tone here is hiding his own deep reservations about universal suffrage, even as he tells Carlyle to "Spare those spasms of dread and disgust."[20] Whitman sees the "only course eligible" as the swallowing of the "big and bitter pill" of Carlyle's "Swarm-ery." He does not directly mention blacks again, though they are implicitly included in his disdainful embrace of the new masses: "By all odds, my friend, the thing to do is to make a flank movement, surround them, disarm them, give them their first degree, incorporate them in the State as voters, and then—wait for the next emergency" (*PW* 2:750). Whit-man goes on to tell Carlyle that his "comic-painful hulla-baloo" is worse than the primitive cries of those whom the new suffrage will be recognizing as citizens—Whitman says he "never yet encountered" such "vituperative cat-squalling . . . not even in extremest hour of midnight, in whooping Tennessee revival, or Bedlam let loose in crowded, colored Carolina bush-meeting" (*PW* 2:750). Apparently aware that his edgy and emotionally uncontrolled outburst here was betraying more than he felt comfortable with, he simply removed the whole passage from the book version of *Democratic Vistas*. Even ten years later, he was still reeling from Carlyle's essay, unsure how to answer it, unsure even that it needed to be answered: "Who cares that he wrote about . . . 'Shooting Niagara' and 'the Nigger Question,'—and didn't at all admire our United States? (I doubt if he ever thought or said half as bad words about us as we deserve)" (*PW* 1:250).

So, while Whitman says he will not "gloss over" the issue of universal suffrage, in the final version of *Democratic Vistas*, that is exactly what he does: he discusses equality between the sexes, but after obliquely raising the issues of race in the opening pages, the essay veers away, never to return, except in some small-print notes at the end, notes that he did not republish with *Democratic Vistas* after the initial printing, moving them instead to his "Notes Left Over" in his collected prose. It is a stunning avoidance, especially given the "anger" Whitman claims he felt when he read Carlyle's harangue, and we hear all the more loudly Whitman's admission, in his footnote on Carlyle, that he "had more than once been in the like mood, during which [Carlyle's] essay was evidently cast, and seen persons and things in the same light, (indeed some might say there are signs of the same feeling in this book)."

Whitman was far from alone in his deep reservations about giving the right to vote to the recently freed slaves. American magazines in the late 1860s and early 1870s were full of Carlyle-like concerns about the extension of the vote to African American males, though usually these views were expressed in less incendiary language than Carlyle's. Some commentators felt constrained by what they considered to be an early version of "political correctness," as if it had come to be considered improper in some quarters even to question the wisdom of black suffrage. "It is a remarkable fact that, in the United States, where more is said in a gratulatory strain about the unrestrained liberty of the press than in any other civilized nation, the force that we call public opinion prevents the open discussion of certain subjects in a degree almost despotic," wrote one commentator in the *Round Table* in 1868: "There is plenty of talk about the heinousness of slavery, about the rights of women, the misgovernment of cities, the corruption of officials, the spread of intemperance, the social evil, and many other subjects whose treatment is pretty certain in some quarters or other to be more or less disagreeable; but we seldom, if ever, hear any one say that the prime dogma of democracy may possibly be unsound; that, at all events, it ought to be subjected to rigorous examination, and tested by all recent and present, as well as by all former, available experience; that the enormous influx of ignorant immigration, together with the proposed enfranchisement of an entire race, late a servile and now scarcely a semi-civilized one, is threatening the republic with dangers far greater than those of the darkest days of the Revolution or of the late disastrous civil war." Democracy itself is on trial with this headlong extension of the right to vote, argued this writer, and if black males get the right to vote, then white females will follow, then black females, and "thus we shall arrive at not universal, but adult suffrage, excluding only minors, lunatics, and perhaps paupers." What will be the effect on democracy of such an all-embracing plebiscite? Politicians will begin to act "with a view not to what is right, pure, elevated in morals or aesthetics, but to what will best tickle the ears of the mob," because "in proportion as suffrage is extended downward the amount of ignorance and prejudice in the aggregate voting body is increased, with the direct consequence that politicians will become more and more demagogues—men who appeal to ignorance and prejudice and not to knowledge and reason."[21]

Some recently discovered manuscripts indicate that Whitman may have started out with the intention of using *Democratic Vistas* to break his silence on the race and suffrage question, and the evidence is that, had he done so, he would have sounded very much like the *Round Table* commentator, but with the added twist that somehow time would take care of the problem. In one manuscript, perhaps notes for a section of *Democratic Vistas* that he never wrote, Whitman counseled himself to "Make a full and plain spoken statement of *the South*—encouraging—the south will yet come up—the blacks must either filter through in time or gradually eliminate & disappear, which is most likely though that termination is far off, or else must so develop in mental and moral qualities and in all the attributes of a leading and dominant race, (which I do not think likely)."[22] Here Whitman sounds indeed like he sees "things in the same light" as Carlyle, predicting the same eventual disappearance of the black race (such applications of evolutionary theory to the prophecy that the Negro race was "destined to disappear in the South" were common in the postwar years)[23] and expressing some contempt for the notion that the black race could progress enough to hold an equal place in American society.

Another Whitman manuscript from around the same time (it refers to the "Acts of Congress" and the "Constitutional Amendments" that Whitman was then attending the debates on) reveals a similar faith that evolutionary laws would solve America's race problem, that all the talk ("the tender appeals") about suffrage and equality would give way to the inexorable laws of "Ethnological Science" that settle "these things by evolution, by natural selection by certain races, notwithstanding all the frantic pages of the sentimentalists, helplessly disappearing [when brought in contact with other races, and] by the slow, sure progress of laws, through sufficient periods of time."[24] George M. Frederickson in *The Black Image in the White Mind* has delineated in detail the various theories of race that "ethnological scientists" came up with in the nineteenth century, and, at one point or another, Whitman seems to have subscribed to most of them. But his evolutionary stance in these manuscript notes suggests that at the time of Reconstruction, he believed the problems of race would eventually vanish, not as blacks became fully functioning citizens, but rather as blacks "filtered out" or disappeared or—less likely—became, through amalgamation, white.

Finally, in an essay he published in 1874, Whitman offered his most direct statement about black suffrage, but then—as he did with the black suffrage passages in the *Democratic Vistas* essay—he removed the key passage before reprinting the essay:

> As if we had not strained the voting and digestive calibre of American Democracy to the utmost for the last fifty years with the millions of ignorant foreigners, we have now infused a powerful percentage of blacks, with about as much intellect and calibre (in the mass) as so many baboons. But we stood the former trial—solved it—and, though this is much harder, will, I doubt not, triumphantly solve this. (*PW* 2:762)

It is difficult to figure out what to make of this passage. Whitman seems once again to express some sort of faith that the future will simply take care of the problem, presumably either by improving the quality of black Americans or by filtering them out of existence. It is not an edifying passage, but it is consistent with a number of comments Whitman made in his later years. His close friendship with W. D. O'Connor ended in 1872 (they basically broke off communications for a decade), apparently over an intense argument about Whitman's obstinate refusal to embrace black suffrage and to show more compassion for the plight of former slaves. By 1888, he was capable of comments like the following to his disciple Horace Traubel, who had asked Whitman his views on racial amalgamation: "I don't believe in it—it is not possible. The nigger, like the Injun, will be eliminated: it is the law of history, races, what-not: always so far inexorable—always to be. Someone proves that a superior grade of rats comes and then all the minor rats are cleared out" (*WWWC* 2:283). In the final year of his life, he was still arguing "that the horror of slavery was not in what it did for the nigger but in what it produced of the whites," and he was quick to propose that the reason "niggers are the happiest people on the earth" is "because they're so damned vacant" (*WWWC* 8:439). Perhaps more dispiriting is Whitman's late affiliation with the South, as if he is still speaking for the slave masters but no longer for the slaves or certainly for the freed slaves:

> I know not how others may feel but to me the South— the old true South, & its succession & presentation the New true South after all outstanding Virginia and the Carolinas, Georgia—is yet inexpressibly dear.—To night I would say one word for that South—the whites. I do not wish to say one word and will not say one word against the blacks—but the blacks can never be to me what the whites are. Below all political relations, even the deepest, are still deeper, personal, physiological and *emotional* ones, the whites are my brothers & I love them. (*NUPM* 2160)

Like virtually all such statements by Whitman, these are "off the record"—either unpublished, excised from the book versions of the essays, or recorded only in conversations. He kept such statements out of his enduring books, almost as if he recognized his own retrogressive position on race, as if he remembered the earlier days of the first three editions of *Leaves*, when he had been more progressive, even radical in his notions of crossing racial boundaries. It is in large part because Whitman was wise enough to keep such views private and not to infect his published work with them that his reputation is preserved today as the absorptive and democratic embracer of American diversity—as the poet who looked for ways to absorb difference rather than eliminate difference. It is as if he knew that his own personal racial biases had no place in work that was looking toward a transformed democratic future, when such biases would presumably be a thing of the past. By keeping his racial views out of *Democratic Vistas*, then, and by muting his direct response to Carlyle's racist comments, Whitman managed to produce an enduring essay that can still be read as a relevant critique of American culture today.

In the fall of 1867, it seemed that everyone was reading and talking about "Shooting Niagara," and so it is no accident that in September of 1867, within a month of the American publication of Carlyle's essay, Whitman wrote to William Conant Church and Francis Pharcellus Church, the editors of the *Galaxy* magazine, letting them know he was writing "an article, (prose,) of some length—the subject opportune—I shall probably name it *Democracy*" (*C* 1:338). The Churches had founded the *Galaxy* in 1866 as a lively alternative to magazines like the *Atlantic Monthly* and *Harper's Monthly* that had become predictable in content and regional in scope; the Churches wanted their new publication to be what Robert Scholnick has called "a truly national magazine, hospitable to the thought of every section."[25] Over the twelve years of its existence, the *Galaxy* regularly published Mark Twain and Henry James, among other well-known writers and cultural figures like General George Custer, whose memoirs they were publishing when he was killed at Little Big Horn. Setting out to create a daring and experimental journal, the Churches embraced Whitman at the urging of Whitman's ardent disciple, the writer W. D. O'Connor. The *Galaxy* published four of Whitman's poems, as well as (in one of their first issues) John Burroughs's essay on Whitman's *Drum-Taps* and (in one of their last) Joaquin Miller's celebratory poem "To Walt Whitman."[26]

The Church brothers must have been pleased, then, to hear from Whitman that he was writing an article that was in fact national in scope and provocative. Whitman told the Churches his essay was "in some respects a rejoinder to" Carlyle's "Shooting Niagara," and he boldly suggested top billing: "I would propose it to you for a leading article for January '68 *Galaxy*." In the same letter, he offered the Churches a poem, then called "Ethiopia Commenting," later titled "Ethiopia Saluting the Colors." It is the only poem Whitman wrote after 1860 that focuses on a black figure and that deals directly with the issue of emancipation; told in the voice of a Union soldier serving under General Sherman in Georgia, the poem records the soldier's response to a hundred-year-old slave woman who shakes her "woolly-white and turban'd head" in disbelief at the scene of white soldiers freeing her and her people.[27] The poem, which the Churches accepted but never published, might have indicated to them that Whitman's proposed essay was going to confront the issue of race and the future of blacks in America and answer Carlyle's harangue much more directly than it ended up doing, and they may have been planning to run the poem as a companion to the part of Whitman's study of democracy that confronted the racial issue, a part that, as it turned out, never materialized.

A month later Whitman sent "Democracy" in, reserving the right to use the article later, "as, for instance, issuing it with added Notes, Appendices, &c. in a pamphlet or small book." So already, by October of 1867, Whitman was imagining the book *Democratic Vistas*, and he was understandably anxious to see how the *Galaxy* article would be received: "we can see better how the cat jumps after the article is before the public" (*C* 1:344).

The Churches, anxious to enter their magazine into the

Carlyle debate, published "Democracy" even earlier than Whitman had hoped, and it went before the public in the December 1867 issue. The cat did not jump as high as Whitman had hoped, but there was in fact some immediate if not very heartening response in the periodical press. The newly founded *Nation* magazine, one of the *Galaxy*'s main competitors, dismissed the essay, saying "we are sorry to say that we get very little from it," describing it as "sensational . . . without form and void," merely repeating Whitman's love of "the average man in the manner and with some of the matter with which readers of his poems are familiar" (December 5, 1867, 453). The *Round Table*, however, a magazine that, like the *Galaxy*, had been founded by two brothers eager to create a publication that would bind together the entire nation and generate nonpartisan, nonsectarian, free and open debate on the major issues facing a country torn in half by the Civil War, responded at some length to both Carlyle's "Shooting Niagara" and Whitman's "Democracy."

The anonymous reviewer (all contributors to the *Round Table* remained, by policy, anonymous, so that ideas instead of personalities would be the focus of attention) begins by praising Whitman for offering "probably the best reply to Mr. Carlyle's *Shooting Niagara* which the nature of the case admits." While "Mr. Carlyle has the advantage in square inches of print," Whitman "more than makes up the difference" "in respect of quality, in jangle and gnarliness." But as the reviewer tries to summarize Whitman's argument, whatever enthusiasm he initially had quickly evaporates: "Mr. Whitman is by all odds the more incomprehensible [of the two writers]; he has a more bewildering way of dispensing with subject or with predicate; . . . of giving big letters to People and Humanity and Scheme and Solidarity and These States, and little ones to 'god' and 'holy ghost.'" So, says this reviewer, "the apparent candor of *Democracy* has a queer accompaniment,—that of admitting in one place

inherent blemishes which seem almost fatal to the theory
in whose statement and deduction elsewhere they are entirely ignored." Whitman's fallacious argument—building a
case for the corruption of the American present and then
ignoring that evidence in projecting an idealized American
future—makes the sympathetic reviewer's job difficult: "it
will be seen that the liveliest desire to do justice to Mr. Whitman's argument does not of necessity imply power to do so."
For this reviewer, Whitman remains maddeningly vague
about what the nation is to do about a situation where "The
People" are busy pursuing material gain while leaving the
government to be run by corrupt and venal tyrants: "*How* we
are to be rid of all this Mr. Whitman gives us not a hint,—
merely holding that, some time or other, we are to be rid of
it." The reviewer concludes by offering a haunting image of
the vast gulf between America's sordid present and its ideal
future, the gulf that Whitman fails to explain how the nation
would cross, and which could turn out to be, ominously, not
a gulf at all but a cascading falls: "Meanwhile, in the immediate present, between us and this splendid future, is a great
gulf fixed, seething with the at least tangible and vivid problems that none show us how to escape, and that, unescaped,
threaten to bear us over Niagara."[28] By ending the review
on that note, the reviewer makes it clear that he finds Whitman's democratic hope unsupported and Carlyle's warnings
about democracy's prospects far more convincing.

This review prompted one *Round Table* reader to write a
long letter to the magazine, which published it in two parts
in December 1867 and January 1868. The writer signed his
letter simply "Wayne." Wayne offers an extended comparison of Whitman and Carlyle, finding each of them to be an
extreme case—Carlyle "a believer in tyrants and ruffians"
whose "faith is in the governor, not the governed," Whitman at "the other extreme" with his unbridled faith in "The
People"—but, as is so often the case with extremes, also re-

markably similar: "in the entire field of English literature there are no two writers more marked by the same characteristics, or who would have been so alike in thought as they would have been under the same training, in the same state of society." Each is, claims this reviewer, a self-righteous and self-appointed prophet, and if we would "change their places of birth and abode," we "would have Carlyle a foaming demagogue in America, humoring the very madness of democracy, and Whitman a flunky for divine right in England, bowing and cringing before every strong-handed, 'divinely-appointed' ruffian who tortured the people most and put his foot heaviest upon their necks."

Whitman and Carlyle seem like opposites, then, only because of the different environments in which they were raised, but their fulminating and illogical ways of arguing were the same: "Our difficulty with Mr. Whitman is that he ascribes too much to democracy—is too certain of its permanence. . . . [H]e has thought only superficially upon the subject, and takes for granted everything which is in doubt. He prophesies and does not reason. He sings a song instead of publishing an argument. . . . [H]e epitomizes, as it were, the spirit which has made us vain, over-confident, and has torn us into factions, deluging the land with fratricidal blood." The democracy that Whitman puts so much faith in is in fact fragile and barely formed, Wayne claims, and most of what has been positive about America has been a result of its untapped resources of land; the future about which Whitman offers "his jubilant guffaw" is in fact bleak, since America too will face "the days of overcrowded population" and increased "money greed," and, once the open lands are occupied, there will be no way for the nation to "prevent a reproduction here of the miseries which afflict men elsewhere." Looking around at the ravages of war and the accelerating money worship, Wayne offers his own assessment: "The truth is, democracy is on trial. It has not passed the experimental stage." Whitman, Wayne says, is basically asking the wrong question: "Is not the real question for a philosopher, 'Can we preserve our democracy?' instead of 'What will democracy achieve if preserved?'" Wayne concludes by sounding an alarm: "What is needed is not prophecy, however exalted, obscure, or stage-hero-like in tone; but alarum cries ringing through the land and bidding the people fly to the rescue of imperilled liberty."[29]

The responses in the *Round Table* had certainly challenged Whitman to think more deeply, in his planned follow-up essays, about democracy and how America needed to deal with the threats to its democratic traditions. His manuscript notes from around this time indicate that he had by now laid out plans for a three-part series: "1st Democracy—(already published.) 2nd Personalism including the Conscience-Moral part 3rd To the Literary Classes—the whole Salvation of the future depends upon a new breed of grand Litterateurs—" (*NUPM* 859). By February of 1868, a little more than a month after Wayne's spirited response, Whitman had finished the second article, "Personalism," and he wrote to the Church brothers again, asking them to "print it positively as the leader." "Democracy" had (in Whitman's own terms) at best caused the cat to stir but not to jump, so he now told the Churches that "Personalism" "is, as a literary performance, I think better than that paper—& will arouse more attention." This time, he said, he was offering "the portrait of the ideal American of the future," and he was now apparently taking on Matthew Arnold in addition to Carlyle, "overhaul[ing] the Culture theory, show[ing] its deficiencies, tested by any grand, practical Democratic text" (*C* 2:19). He wrote to Moncure Conway in England to ask him to use whatever influence he had to get the essay published there in the *Fortnightly Review*—the essay was, after all, responding most directly to British writers. "Personalism" appeared in the May 1868 *Galaxy*, this time not as the lead essay, but rather following several other pieces, including, oddly, an essay on "Our Millionaires," listing the millionaires of New York and explaining how each had made his fortune, noting that "ten men now own one-tenth part of the whole taxable property of the city," and raising the question about whether becoming a millionaire might someday be a democratic activity, something available to all instead of to just a few because "to-day the ideal society is one where every man is worth one million of dollars!" Whitman's "Democracy" essay had dealt with the problems of Americans' material-ist fervor and ended up claiming that the nation's money lust was just a temporary stepping-stone to a more satisfy-ing spiritual future. "Personalism" now tried to imagine that future not as a nation of millionaires but an orderly nation of prosperous and thrifty citizens bound by a common pur-pose: "I can conceive such a community organized in run-ning order, powers judiciously delegated, farming, building, trade, courts, mails, schools, elections, all attended to; and then the rest of life, the main thing, freely branching and blossoming in each individual, and bearing golden fruit."[30]

"Personalism" was met with a more deafening silence than "Democracy." Only two brief notes in the *Round Table* acknowledged its appearance. The first called the essay "the second of Walt Whitman's remarkable yawps, entitled this time *Personalism*, and apparently a sequel to his former article about democracy, which it surpasses, if possible, in incoherency and bombastic unreason." The second notice dismissed both of Whitman's essays by arguing that "only the vicious mental habits that invariably spring from con-stant associations with one's intellectual inferiors could possibly lead a man of Whitman's natural powers to ex-pose himself by publishing such inconceivable drivel as his pseudo-political articles. . . . Indeed, such yawps rather re-tard the machine they are meant to accelerate, for the reason that they excite derision instead of admiration—contempt instead of conviction."[31] Whitman sent copies of his essays to various acquaintances but got little response.[32]

Despite the palpable lack of interest, Whitman already had the third and final installment of his prose work done and was still coming up with schemes to keep the Churches' interest, conjuring up a public fervor that existed only in his imagination: "I think it will be best not to delay [publication] too long, as the interest in the thing is now up, something like a serial story." Whitman wanted the third install ment, which was nearly twice as long as either of the first two, to appear in the July *Galaxy*, and suggested that this new essay was "more appropriate & serviceable—more to rouse editorial & critical remark, &c—than the already published articles" (*C* 2:32–33). The Churches were no longer buying it, however, and the third essay, now called "Orbic Literature," was never published as a separate article. Disappointed but undaunted, Whitman over the next two years combined it with revised versions of the two published essays to create *Democratic Vistas*. Within three months of having "Orbic Literature" turned down at the *Galaxy*, Whitman was already writing to his mother about how "I am working at my leisure on my little book": "I dont know whether I have spoken of it before—in prose—those pieces in the *Galaxy* form portions of it—it is on political & literary subjects—It is a real pleasure to me" (*C* 2:39).

After being reduced to paying a job printer, William E. Chapin, to print his 1867 edition of *Leaves of Grass*, the shabbiest and most chaotic of all the editions, and to issuing it sporadically over the next couple of years as he found the funds to bind up a few copies, Whitman was finally able to hook up with J. S. Redfield, a once highly respected New York publisher who had made his reputation in the 1850s by publishing the first complete edition of Edgar Allan Poe's work. Redfield had also at that time been the publisher of Poe's

favorite novelist, the immensely popular Southern writer
William Gilmore Simms, whose proslavery stance Redfield
did not agree with, but whose best-selling novels he liked
a great deal. But Redfield was never a great financial man-
ager, and, like many publishers on the edge of the Civil War
(including Thayer and Eldridge, the publishers of the 1860
edition of *Leaves*), his publishing business failed and in the
fall of 1860 was taken over by one of his assistants. Redfield,
who had published books about and by William Seward, the
presumptive Republican candidate for president in 1860
until the dark horse Lincoln emerged victorious, cashed in
on his service to Seward by seeking and receiving a consul's
position in Italy when Seward became Lincoln's secretary of
state. After returning from Italy and dabbling in the lace-
making business until going bankrupt again,[33] Redfield decided to reenter the publishing world in late 1868. He began
modestly enough, reprinting popular newspaper pieces in
book form, but he soon decided that Whitman, now widely
admired as a person (because of his well-publicized service
in Civil War hospitals) if still very controversial as a writer,
might be a good bet to draw attention to his new publishing
venture. He started by publishing John Burroughs' *Notes
on Walt Whitman as Poet and Person* in an expanded form;
Burroughs' admiring volume (he argues that Whitman is
one of those rare geniuses who "mark out and make new
eras")[34] set the stage for Redfield's breathtaking decision
to publish three of Whitman's books at the same time—a
new edition of *Leaves of Grass*, Whitman's *Passage to India*
(which he then thought of as his new book of poetry that
would be a companion volume to *Leaves*), and *Democratic
Vistas*. Redfield's entire list in 1872 consisted of seventeen
books, and nearly a quarter of them were by or about Whitman. And, perhaps predictably, Redfield once again went
bankrupt and was liquidating his assets by 1873.

Redfield's important involvement in *Democratic Vistas*

underscores how Whitman's book, while very much a product of his life in the nation's capital, is also a book emerging from his native environs in and around New York City.
From the time he approached the Church brothers about his
"Democracy" essay in the fall of 1867, he was spending extended periods of time in New York while taking leaves from
his clerk's position in Washington. He met with the Church
brothers in New York in 1867, and of course the *Galaxy* was
a New York periodical. He was in New York and Brooklyn
in the fall of 1867, stayed there for six weeks in the fall of
1868, a month in late summer of 1869, a couple of weeks in
the spring of 1870, and then again for nearly three months
in the summer and fall of 1870, when he made the arrangements with Redfield for the publication of his three books.
Whitman continued working on *Democratic Vistas* up to the
last minute, recording in his concluding notes the very date
he is "send[ing] my last pages to press," September 19, 1870,
as he is getting news of the demise of Napoleon III in the
Franco-Prussian war, meaning that Louis Napoleon's "rat-
cunning" is finally "at an end," and another country would
be reopening its democratic vistas as the third French republic was already forming. While the essay was composed
over the course of three years, it maintains an up-to-the-
minute feel with so many momentous events—the passage
of the Fifteenth Amendment, the end of the French Empire—happening as the essay is being finished.

Whitman delivered his finished book to Redfield in early
October 1870, and Redfield immediately printed it along
with *Leaves of Grass* and *Passage to India*. All three of the
Redfield Whitman books were originally published in match-
ing paperback editions, and, while there is no indication on
the title pages that Redfield is the publisher, the covers all
prominently feature Redfield's name and address. These are
anomalous covers, since Whitman indicates the "place" for
each book is Washington, D.C., even while simultaneously

indicating the place of publication is New York. *Democratic Vistas* is one of the few books, then, with two distinct locations indicating "place," as if to suggest that, while the book was written in D.C., it still emerged from New York. Even the cover, then, indicated the width of Whitman's vistas, shimmering from the Southern heat of the nation's capital to the Northern cold of its largest city. Redfield printed five hundred copies of *Democratic Vistas* and tried to sell them for seventy-five cents each; he shipped some to an agent in England for possible sales there. Since all three books were appearing near the end of the year, Whitman and Redfield decided to print the date "1871" on the covers to keep the books seeming fresh for the hoped-for sales in the new year, sales that in fact never materialized.

Like so much of his work, *Democratic Vistas* waited for a hundred years before it began to receive the kind of engagement Whitman cried out for, before it began to be grappled with by the "athletic" readers that he knew America needed and that he called for in his essay. When the book was originally published, it received only one cursory notice in the United States: The *New York Times* (November 11, 1870) dismissed it as "one of the curiosities of the book world," which, like all of Whitman's books, was "only fit for those who make researches in literature not suited to family reading." Whitman apparently considered dipping into his old bag of tricks and stirring up controversy by writing his own anonymous review of the book, as he had done for the first edition of *Leaves of Grass*: he left behind a manuscript in which he calls *Democratic Vistas* a "tremendous & electric pamphlet."[35] Whitman now lacked his old connections in the press, however, and the self-review was never published.

The first intelligent and enthusiastic responses to the book came from across the Atlantic, where Whitman had been gaining fame and followers ever since the respected

English literary figure William Michael Rossetti issued an expurgated selection of Whitman's poems in 1868. The *Sunderland Times* (May 21, 1872) began its review of *Democratic Vistas* with these words: "An original thinker on the other side of the Atlantic, the magnanimous Walt Whitman, has lately been looking through democratic vistas. Having mastered the lessons of the past as much as any man, and scanned the present with a remarkably keen eye, he has turned his telescope on the future and sees visions there that we trust will by and by be realised." This notice appeared nearly a year after a thoughtful, expansive essay on Whitman's work by the Irish scholar Edward Dowden in the July 1871 issue of the *Westminster Review*, in which Dowden effectively captured Whitman's oscillating disgust with and hope for the American democratic spirit: "A vast and more and more thoroughly appointed body Whitman finds in the American world, and little or no soul. His senses are flattered, his imagination roused and delighted by the vast movement of life which surrounds him, its outward glory and gladness, but when he inquires, What is behind all this? the answer is of the saddest and most shameful kind." Dowden notes that some of Whitman's assessments of America in fact sound very much like Carlyle's, but always with a key difference: "Such a picture of the outcome of American democracy is ugly enough to satisfy the author of 'Shooting Niagara—and after?' but such a picture only represents the worst side of the life of great cities. Whitman can behold these things, not without grief, not without shame, but without despair. . . . He takes account of the evil anxiously, accurately; and can still rejoice. Upon the whole his spirit is exulting and prompt in cheerful action; not self-involved, dissatisfied, and fed by indignation." While Carlyle wails, despairs, and prepares for civilization to tumble to its ultimate destruction, Whitman characteristically finds hope, a vista.

This enthusiasm for Whitman in Britain and Ireland inspired a young Welshman named Ernest Rhys to write to the poet and propose bringing his works out in cheap British editions that would reach the British working class and would begin to develop in them democratic attitudes. Such an edition, Rhys promised Whitman, would put Whitman's work "in the reach of the poorest member of the great social democracy. . . . I am sure you will be tremendously glad to help us here, and in the very camp of the enemy, the stronghold of caste and aristocracy, and all selfishness between rich and poor!"[36] It is ironic that *Democratic Vistas* became far more widely known in the United Kingdom than in the United States. In 1887, Rhys helped get *Democratic Vistas, and Other Papers* published in the Walter Scott Publishing Company's popular Canterbury Series, with a preface by Whitman affirming his "theory" that "the bulk, the common people of all civilized nations" deserve access to "Enlightenment, Democracy and Fair-Show." The book was regularly reprinted for the next five years. *Democratic Vistas* also appeared in a Danish edition, translated by Rudolf Schmidt as *Demokratiske Fremblik*, in 1874.

While the essay was being read in Britain and Denmark, where its projection of a reconstructed democratic future resonated more strongly than in the United States, it faded into obscurity in America. After its initial U.S. appearance in paperback in 1871, the essay would never again during Whitman's lifetime appear in his own country in a book bearing its title. Whitman quickly began to give up on the idea that *Democratic Vistas* would have a lasting impact on his nation: in 1872 he wrote to Edward Dowden that the essay "remains quite unread, uncalled for, here in America," and to Rudolf Schmidt he reported that "it is at present in danger of falling still-born here" (*J* 2:152, 154). But right through to the end of his life, he nonetheless insisted that "to know me to the full," his readers "must not know only the poems, but the story there in prose, too—'Democratic Vistas,' certainly, if none other" (*WWWC* 6:376).

So Whitman never abandoned the essay. He bound the leftover printed sheets of the essay in his *Two Rivulets* for the American Centennial in 1876, then kept tinkering with the piece, inserting a new opening paragraph in which he evoked John Stuart Mill, adding him to Arnold and Carlyle as the British essayists he proposed to engage in *Democratic Vistas*, dropping his concluding notes, altering some spellings, changing some words, and reformatting the paragraphs. Though he was never sure his changes improved the essay ("I have never been able to settle it with myself," he said in 1888, whether his revisions were "an improvement or not: often the first instinct is the best instinct" [*WWWC* 3:132]), he included his revised version in his *Specimen Days and Collect* in 1882, where it took its place permanently tucked away deep in his collected prose.

As we have seen, most early commentators viewed Whitman's ideas about democracy as either vague or naive or both, but more recent critics—including political scientists—have found his thinking about the issue to be complex, serious, and illuminating. In 1990, in the journal *Political Theory*, major political theorists debated Whitman's concepts of democracy, and George Kateb called him "perhaps the greatest philosopher of the culture of democracy."[37] Morton Schoolman has focused on Whitman in *Reason and Horror*, his book-length study of "critical theory, democracy, and aesthetic individuality."[38] And Frank Jason in a 2007 article in *Review of Politics*, argues strongly for "Whitman's significance to contemporary political theory" as a "theorist of the democratic sublime."[39]

As with almost everything that Whitman wrote, the disagreements about the meaning of *Democratic Vistas* are intense and striking. This is, after all, the poet who asked "Do I contradict myself?" and confidently answered his own question by saying, "Very well then I contradict myself, / (I am large, I contain multitudes)." Since Whitman built his writing on maintaining the contradictions (and setting up a dynamic) between strength and hope, the individual and the en masse, pride and sympathy, the United States (the historically contingent nation) and America (the idealized democratic nation), there was always the risk that he would be read partially, heard simply as the poet of strength, individuality, pride, and the United States, *or* simply as the poet of hope, camaraderie, sympathy, and something more inclusive than the United States that he called America. So, while a liberal voice like Cornel West—arguing that for Whitman "democracy had deep ontological, existential and social implications"—can find *Democratic Vistas* "a classic in the defense of individuality and social justice,"[40] a conservative voice like David Brooks can argue just as strenuously that "Whitman got America right" in *Democratic Vistas* because "in the end, he accepted his country's 'extreme business energy,' its 'almost maniacal appetite for wealth.' He knew that the country's dreams were all built upon that energy and drive, and eventually the spirit of commercial optimism would always prevail."[41] It is always easy to latch onto one side of the intricately balanced contradictory tensions—is the United States dedicated to assuring "social justice" or to guaranteeing that "energy and drive" will be rewarded with "wealth"?—that Whitman argued formed the very sinews of the nation, but it is ultimately more rewarding to play the role of Whitman's "athletic" reader—the reader he calls for in *Democratic Vistas*—and to grapple with his meanings, never settling on any simplistic answer to the contradictory impulses that generated and still sustain America. He is the poet who at once celebrates the rights of the individual and the rights of the diverse multitude; the poet who celebrates strength while embracing the weak: "the poet of slaves and of the masters of slaves" (*NUPM* 1:67).[42] *Democratic Vistas* still offers today's readers the opportunity to argue with Whitman over the nature of democracy and the future of the nation.

NOTES

1. The next several paragraphs are adapted from my essay on Whitman's democracy in *WWE*, 171–174.

2. William Tindall, "A Sketch of Mayor Sayles J. Bowen," *Records of the Columbia Historical Society, Washington, D.C.*, 18 (1915), 30–36.

3. See Tindall, 25–43.

4. W. T. Bandy, "An Unknown 'Washington Letter' by Walt Whitman," *Walt Whitman Quarterly Review* 2 (Winter 1985), 25.

5. Whitman was hardly alone in this doubting. See David Blight, *Race and Reunion: The Civil War in American Memory* (Cambridge: Harvard University Press, 2001): "The forces of reconciliation overwhelmed the emancipationist vision in the national culture," erasing the intense ideological battle over slavery that initiated the war and leading to a neglect of the challenges of dealing with the huge number of freed African Americans (2, 57).

6. See my analysis of how Whitman forgot to answer Carlyle in "Lucifer and Ethiopia: Whitman, Race, and Poetics before the Civil War and After," 77–80. The note on suffrage can be found in *Democratic Vistas*, 83.

7. See *PW* 2:531.

8. See "Paying the 1st U. S. C. T.," *PW* 2:587, and "Last of the War Cases," *PW* 2:625–626.

9. See Cornell W. Clayton, *The Politics of Justice: The Attorney General and the Making of Legal Policy* (Armonk, New York: M. E. Sharpe, 1992), 19–22.

10. Richard Gid Powers, *Broken: The Troubled Past and Uncertain Future of the FBI* (New York: Simon and Schuster, 2004), 40–42.

11. Nathaniel C. Towle, *A History and Analysis of the Constitution of the United States, . . . with Papers and Tables Illustrative of the Action of the Government and the People Under It* (Boston: Little, Brown, 1860), 382.

12. Horace Greeley, *The Tribune Almanac for the Years 1838 to 1868, Inclusive* (New York: New York *Tribune*, 1868), 39.

13. *Revised Statutes of the United States* (Washington: Government Printing Office, 1875), 58–59. Today's Department of Justice, in contrast, has well over one hundred thousand employees.

14. Terry Eagleton, "The Critic as Partisan: William Hazlitt's Radical Imagination," *Harper's* (April 2009), 77.

15. "The Literary World," *J* 2:89.

16. See Floyd Stovall, *The Foreground of Leaves of Grass* (Charlottesville: University Press of Virginia, 1974), 110.

17. Walt Whitman, *I Sit and Look Out: Editorials from the Brooklyn Daily Times*, ed. Emory Holloway and Vernolian Schwarz (New York: Columbia University Press, 1932), 68.

18. Gary Schmidgall, ed., *Intimate with Walt: Selections from Whitman's Conversations with Horace Traubel, 1888–1892* (Iowa City: University of Iowa Press, 2001), 166, 203.

19. Thomas Carlyle, "Shooting Niagara: and After?" *Macmillans Magazine* 16 (August 1867), 319–320.

20. Luke Mancuso in *The Strange Sad War Revolving* hears Whitman's tone in this passage as "satiric" and believes that Whitman "neutralizes" Carlyle's "racism through satire"; he also suggests that Whitman's later deletion of the passage simply indicates that he found the whole argument "anachronistic because of the successful ratification of the Fifteenth Amendment in 1870" (74–75).

21. "Democracy on Trial," *Round Table* (February 15, 1868), 160.

22. Kenneth M. Price, "Whitman's Solutions to 'The Problem of the Blacks,'" *Resources for American Literary Study* 15 (Autumn 1985), 205–208.

23. See George Frederickson, *The Black Image in the White Mind* (Middletown, Connecticut: Wesleyan University Press, 1971), 237.

24. Geoffrey Sill, "Whitman on 'The Black Question': A New Manuscript," *Walt Whitman Quarterly Review* 8 (Fall 1990), 69–75.

25. Robert J. Scholnick, "*The Galaxy* and American Democratic Culture, 1866–1878," *Journal of American Studies* 16 (1982), 71.

26. Edward Chielens, "*The Galaxy*," in Edward E. Chielens, ed., *American Literary Magazines* (New York: Greenwood, 1986), 139–144.

27. See my reading of this poem in relation to *Democratic Vistas* in "Lucifer and Ethiopia."

28. "Walt Whitman's Utopia," *Round Table* (December 7, 1867), 370–371.

29. Wayne, "Democracy, Carlyle, and Whitman," *Round Table* (December 21, 1867), 413–414; and (January 11, 1868), 22–23.

30. "Personalism," *Galaxy* (May 1868), 546.

31. *Round Table* (April 25, 1868), 268; (May 16, 1868), 316.

32. Bronson Alcott did respond enthusiastically and noted in his journal on April 28, 1868, that he had "read 'Personalism' again after a day's work. Verily, great grand doctrine, and great grand Walt. . . . Another American beside Thoreau and Emerson" (quoted in Gay Wilson Allen, *Walt Whitman Handbook*, 296).

33. "In Bankruptcy," *Brooklyn Daily Eagle* (August 6, 1868), 4.

34. John Burroughs, *Notes on Walt Whitman as Poet and Person*, 2nd ed. (New York: J. S. Redfield, 1871), 3.

35. William White, "Whitman's *Democratic Vistas*: An Unpublished Self-Review?" *American Book Collector* 16 (December 1965), 21.

36. *WWWC* 1:452.

37. George Kateb, "Walt Whitman and the Culture of Democracy," *Political Theory* 18 (1990), 545–571; with responses to Kateb from David Bromwich, Nancy L. Rosenblum, Michael Mosher, and Leo Marx.

38. Morton Schoolman, *Reason and Horror: Critical Theory, Democracy, and Aesthetic Individuality* (New York: Routledge, 2001).

39. Frank Jason, "Aesthetic Democracy: Walt Whitman and the Poetry of the People," *Review of Politics* 69 (June 2007), 402–430.

40. Cornel West, "On Walt Whitman," *The Cornel West Reader* (New York: Basic Civitas Books, 1999), 489–491.

41. David Brooks, "The Commercial Republic," *New York Times* (March 17, 2009). Brooks has used *Democratic Vistas* to support a number of his own political views. In the May 2003 *Atlantic*, Brooks published a piece called "What Whitman Knew," timed to appear just as President George W. Bush was declaring an end to combat operations in Iraq in front of a giant "Mission Accomplished" banner. In that essay, Brooks read *Democratic Vistas* as a kind of apologia for the neocon policy that believed the United States could force democracy on a grateful Iraq, which, during weeks of relentless bombings, so we were told, would lie back and enjoy it, eventually showering American soldiers with flowers: "No one since Whitman has captured quite so well the motivating hopefulness that propels American policy and makes

the nation a great and restless force in the world." Whitman's work, in Brooks's view, could help Americans deal with the sting of having lost the sympathy of the world and having become, in the year and a half since 9/11, despised internationally: "Whitman's essay, with its nuanced understanding of the American national character, stands today as a powerful rebuttal to, for example, the parades of European anti-Americans. What these groups despise is a cliché—a flat and simple-minded image of American power. They do not see, as Whitman did, that despite its many imperfections, America is a force for democracy and progress." So, Brooks says, despite "its hodgepodge nature," *Democratic Vistas* is "our nation's most brilliant political sermon because it embodies the exuberant energy of American society—the energy that can make other peoples so nervous." *Atlantic Monthly* (May 2003), 32–33.

42. See my essay, "'What a Filthy Presidentiad!': Clinton's Whitman, Bush's Whitman, and Whitman's America," *Virginia Quarterly Review* 81 (Spring 2005), 96–113, for an exploration of these tensions in Whitman's definition of the "United States" and "America."

DEMOCRATIC

VISTAS.

Electrotyped by SMITH & McDOUGAL, 82 Beekman Street, New York.

DEMOCRATIC VISTAS.

AMERICA, filling the present with greatest deeds and problems, cheerfully accepting the past, including Feudalism, (as, indeed, the present is but the legitimate birth of the past, including feudalism,) counts, as I reckon, for her justification and success, (for who, as yet, dare claim success?) almost entirely on the future. Nor is that hope unwarranted. To-day, ahead, though dimly yet, we see, in vistas, a copious, sane, gigantic offspring.

For our New World I consider far less important for what it has done, or what it is, than for results to come. Sole among nationalities, These States have assumed the task to put in forms of lasting power and practicality, on areas of amplitude rivaling the operations of the physical kosmos, the moral and political speculations of ages, long, long deferred, the Democratic Republican principle, and the theory of development and perfection by voluntary standards, and self-suppliance. Who else, indeed, except the United States, in history, so far, have accepted in unwitting faith, and, as we now see, stand, act upon, and go security for, these things?

But let me strike at once the key-note of my purpose in the following strain. First premising that, though passages of it have been written at widely different times, (it is, in fact, a collection of memoranda, perhaps for future designers, comprehenders,) and though it may be open to the charge of one part contradicting another—for there are opposite sides to the great question of Democracy, as to every great question—I feel

the parts harmoniously blended in my own realization
and convictions, and present them to be read only in
such oneness, each page modified and tempered by the
others.   Bear in mind, too, that they are not the result
of studying up in political economy, but of the ordinary
sense, observing, wandering among men, These States,
these stirring years of war and peace.   I will not gloss
over the appalling dangers of universal suffrage in the
United States.   In fact, it is to admit and face these
dangers I am writing.   To him or her within whose
thought rages the battle, advancing, retreating, between Democracy's convictions, aspirations, and the
People's crudeness, vice, caprices, I mainly write this
book.

I shall use the words America and Democracy as con-
vertible terms.   Not an ordinary one is the issue.   The
United States are destined either to surmount the gorgeous history of Feudalism, or else prove the most tremendous failure of time.   Not the least doubtful am I
on any prospects of their material success.   The triumphant future of their business, geographic, and productive departments, on larger scales and in more varieties
than ever, is certain.   In those respects the Republic
must soon (if she does not already) outstrip all examples hitherto afforded, and dominate the world.*

---

* "From a territorial area of less than nine hundred thousand square miles, the Union has expanded into over four millions and a half—fifteen times larger than that of Great Britain
and France combined—with a shore-line, including Alaska, equal
to the entire circumference of the earth, and with a domain
within these lines far wider than that of the Romans in their
proudest days of conquest and renown.   With a river, lake, and
coastwise commerce estimated at over two thousand millions of
dollars per year; with a railway traffic of four to six thousand
millions per year, and the annual domestic exchanges of the
country running up to nearly ten thousand millions per year;
with over two thousand millions of dollars invested in manufacturing, mechanical, and mining industry; with over five hundred millions of acres of land in actual occupancy, valued, with
their appurtenances, at over seven thousand millions of dollars,
and producing annually crops valued at over three thousand millions of dollars; with a realm which, if the density of Belgium's

Admitting all this, with the priceless value of our political institutions, general suffrage (and cheerfully acknowledging the latest, widest opening of the doors,) I say that, far deeper than these, what finally and only is to make of our Western World a Nationality superior to any hitherto known, and outtopping the past, must be vigorous, yet unsuspected Literatures, perfect personalities and sociologies, original, transcendental, and expressing (what, in highest sense, are not yet expressed at all,) Democracy and the Modern. With these, and out of these, I promulge new races of Teachers, and of perfect Women, indispensable to endow the birth-stock of a New World. For Feudalism, caste, the Ecclesiastic traditions, though palpably retreating from political institutions, still hold essentially, by their spirit, even in this country, entire possession of the more important fields, indeed the very subsoil, of education, and of social standards and Literature.

I say that Democracy can never prove itself beyond cavil, until it founds and luxuriantly grows its own forms of arts, poems, schools, theology, displacing all that exists, or that has been produced anywhere in the past, under opposite influences.

It is curious to me that while so many voices, pens, minds, in the press, lecture-rooms, in our Congress, &c., are discussing intellectual topics, pecuniary dangers, legislative problems, the suffrage, tariff and labor questions, and the various business and benevolent needs of America, with propositions, remedies, often worth deep attention, there is one need, a hiatus, and the profoundest, that no eye seems to perceive, no voice to state. Our fundamental want to-day in the United States, with closest, amplest reference to pres-

---

population were possible, would be vast enough to include all the present inhabitants of the world; and with equal rights guaranteed to even the poorest and humblest of our forty millions of people—we can, with a manly pride akin to that which distinguished the palmiest days of Rome, claim," &c., &c., &c. — *Vice-President Colfax's Speech, July* 4, 1870.

ent conditions, and to the future, is of a class, and the
clear idea of a class, of native Authors, Literatuses, far
different, far higher in grade than any yet known,
sacerdotal, modern, fit to cope with our occasions,
lands, permeating the whole mass of American mentality, taste, belief, breathing into it a new breath of
life, giving it decision, affecting politics far more than
the popular superficial suffrage, with results inside
and underneath the elections of Presidents or Con-
gresses, radiating, begetting appropriate teachers and
schools, manners, costumes, and, as its grandest result, accomplishing, (what neither the schools nor the
churches and their clergy have hitherto accomplished,
and without which this nation will no more stand, permanently, soundly, than a house will stand without a
substratum,) a religious and moral character beneath
the political and productive and intellectual bases of
The States. For know you not, dear, earnest reader,
that the people of our land may all know how to read
and write, and may all possess the right to vote—and
yet the main things may be entirely lacking?—(and this
to supply or suggest them.)

Viewed, to-day, from a point of view sufficiently overarching, the problem of humanity all over the civilized
world is social and religious, and is to be finally met
and treated by literature. The priest departs, the divine Literatus comes. Never was anything more wanted
than, to-day, and here in The States, the Poet of the
Modern is wanted, or the great Literatus of the Modern. At all times, perhaps, the central point in any
nation, and that whence it is itself really swayed the
most, and whence it sways others, is its national literature, especially its archetypal poems. Above all previous lands, a great original literature is surely to become the justification and reliance, (in some respects
the sole reliance,) of American Democracy.

Few are aware how the great literature penetrates
all, gives hue to all, shapes aggregates and individuals,
and, after subtle ways, with irresistible power, constructs, sustains, demolishes at will. Why tower, in

reminiscence, above all the old nations of the earth, two special lands, petty in themselves, yet inexpressibly gigantic, beautiful, columnar? Immortal Judah lives, and Greece immortal lives, in a couple of poems.

Nearer than this. It is not generally realized, but it is true, as the genius of Greece, and all the sociology, personality, politics and religion of those wonderful states, resided in their literature or esthetics, that what was afterwards the main support of European chivalry, the feudal, ecclesiastical, dynastic world over there, forming its osseous structure, holding it together for hundreds, thousands of years, preserving its flesh and bloom, giving it form, decision, rounding it out, and so saturating it in the conscious and unconscious blood, breed, belief, and intuitions of men, that it still prevails powerfully to this day, in defiance of the mighty changes of time, was its literature, permeating to the very marrow, especially that major part, its enchanting songs, ballads, and poems.*

To the ostent of the senses and eyes, I know, the influences which stamp the world's history are wars, uprisings or downfalls of dynasties, changeful movements of trade, important inventions, navigation, military or civil governments, advent of powerful personalities, conquerors, &c. These of course play their part; yet, it may be, a single new thought, imagination, principle, even literary style, fit for the time, put in shape by some great Literatus, and projected among man-

---

* See, for hereditaments, specimens, Walter Scott's Border Minstrelsy, Percy's Collection, Ellis's Early English Metrical Romances, the European Continental Poems of Walter of Aquitania, and the Nibelungen, of pagan stock, but monkish-feudal redaction; the history of the Troubadours, by Fauriel; even the far, far back cumbrous old Hindu epics, as indicating the Asian eggs, out of which European chivalry was hatched; Ticknor's chapters on the Cid, and on the Spanish poems and poets of Calderon's time. Then always, and, of course, as the superbest, poetic culmination-expression of Feudalism, the Shaksperean dramas, in the attitudes, dialogue, characters, &c., of the princes, lords and gentlemen, the pervading atmosphere, the implied and expressed standard of manners, the high port and proud stomach, the regal embroidery of style, &c.

kind, 'may duly cause changes, growths, removals,
greater than the longest and bloodiest war, or the
most stupendous merely political, dynastic, or commercial overturn.

In short, as, though it may not be realized, it is
strictly true, that a few first-class poets, philosophs,
and authors, have substantially settled and given status
to the entire religion, education, law, sociology, &c., of
the hitherto civilized world, by tinging and often creating the atmospheres out of which they have arisen,
such also must stamp, and more than ever stamp, the
interior and real Democratic construction of this American continent, to-day, and days to come.

Remember also this fact of difference, that, while
through the antique and through the mediæval ages,
highest thoughts and ideals realized themselves, and
their expression made its way by other arts, as much
as, or even more than by, technical literature, (not open
to the mass of persons, nor even to the majority of
eminent persons;) such literature in our day and for
current purposes, is not only more eligible than all the
other arts put together, but has become the only general means of morally influencing the world. Painting, sculpture, and the dramatic theatre, it would
seem, no longer play an indispensable or even important part in the workings and mediumship of intellect, utility, or even high esthetics. Architecture
remains, doubtless with capacities, and a real future.
Then music, the combiner, nothing more spiritual, nothing more sensuous, a god, yet completely human, advances, prevails, holds highest place; supplying in certain wants and quarters what nothing else could supply.
Yet, in the civilization of to-day it is undeniable that,
over all the arts, literature dominates, serves beyond
all—shapes the character of church and school—or, at
any rate, is capable of doing so. Including the literature of science, its scope is indeed unparalleled.

Before proceeding further, it were perhaps well to
discriminate on certain points. Literature tills its
crops in many fields, and some may flourish, while
others lag. What I say in these Vistas has its main

bearing on Imaginative Literature, especially Poetry, the stock of all. In the department of Science, and the specialty of Journalism, there appear, in These States, promises, perhaps fulfilments, of highest earnestness, reality, and life. These, of course, are modern. But in the region of imaginative, spinal and essential attributes, something equivalent to creation is imperatively demanded. For not only is it not enough that the new blood, new frame of Democracy shall be vivified and held together merely by political means, superficial suffrage, legislation, &c., but it is clear to me that, unless it goes deeper, gets at least as firm and as warm a hold in men's hearts, emotions and belief, as, in their days, Feudalism or Ecclesiasticism, and inaugurates its own perennial sources, welling from the centre forever, its strength will be defective, its growth doubtful, and its main charm wanting.

I suggest, therefore, the possibility, should some two or three really original American poets, (perhaps artists or lecturers,) arise, mounting the horizon like planets, stars of the first magnitude, that, from their eminence, fusing contributions, races, far localities, &c., together, they would give more compaction and more moral identity, (the quality to-day most needed,) to These States, than all its Constitutions, legislative and judicial ties, and all its hitherto political, warlike, or materialistic experiences. As, for instance, there could hardly happen anything that would more serve The States, with all their variety of origins, their diverse climes, cities, standards, &c., than possessing an aggregate of heroes, characters, exploits, sufferings, prosperity or misfortune, glory or disgrace, common to all, typical of all—no less, but even greater would it be to possess the aggregation of a cluster of mighty poets, artists, teachers, fit for us, national expressers, comprehending and effusing for the men and women of The States, what is universal, native, common to all, inland and seaboard, northern and southern. The historians say of ancient Greece, with her ever-jealous autonomies, cities, and states, that the only positive unity she ever owned or received, was the sad unity of a common subjection, at the last, to foreign conquerors. Subjection, aggregation of that sort, is impossible to America; but the fear of conflicting and irreconcilable interiors, and the lack of a common skeleton, knitting all close, continually haunts me. Or, if it does not, nothing is plainer than the need, a long period to come, of a fusion of The States into the only reliable identity, the moral and artistic one. For, I say, the true nationality of The States, the genuine union, when we come to a mortal crisis, is, and is to be, after all, neither the written law, nor, (as is generally supposed,) either self-interest, or common pecuniary or material objects—but the fervid and tremendous IDEA, melting everything else with resistless heat, and solving all lesser and definite distinctions in vast, indefinite, spiritual, emotional power.

It may be claimed, (and I admit the weight of the claim,) that common and general worldly prosperity, and a populace well-to-do, and with all life's material comforts, is the main thing, and is enough. It may be argued that our Republic is, in performance, really enacting to-day the grandest arts, poems, &c., by beating up the wilderness into fertile farms, and in her railroads, ships, machinery, &c. And it may be asked, Are these not better, indeed, for America, than any utterances even of greatest rhapsode, artist, or literatus?

I too hail those achievements with pride and joy: then answer that the soul of man will not with such only—nay, not with such at all—be finally satisfied; but needs what, (standing on those and on all things, as the feet stand on the ground,) is addressed to the loftiest, to itself alone.

Out of such considerations, such truths, arises for treatment in these Vistas the important question of Character, of an American stock-personality, with Literatures and Arts for outlets and return-expressions, and, of course, to correspond, within outlines common to all. To these, the main affair, the thinkers of the United States, in general so acute, have either given feeblest attention, or have remained, and remain, in a state of somnolence.

For my part, I would alarm and caution even the political and business reader, and to the utmost extent, against the prevailing delusion that the establishment of free political institutions, and plentiful intellectual smartness, with general good order, physical plenty, industry, &c., (desirable and precious advantages as they all are,) do, of themselves, determine and yield to our experiment of Democracy the fruitage of success. With such advantages at present fully, or almost fully, possessed—the Union just issued, victorious, from the struggle with the only foes it need ever fear, (namely, those within itself, the interior ones,) and with unprecedented materialistic advancement—Society, in These States, is cankered, crude, superstitious, and rotten. Political, or law-made society is, and private, or voluntary society, is also. In any vigor, the element of the moral conscience, the most important, the vertebræ, to State or man, seems to me either entirely lacking or seriously enfeebled or ungrown.

I say we had best look our time and lands searchingly in the face, like a physician diagnosing some deep disease. Never was there, perhaps, more hollowness at heart than at present, and here in the United States. Genuine belief seems to have left us. The underlying principles of The States are not honestly believed in, (for all this hectic glow, and these melo-dramatic screamings,) nor is Humanity itself believed in. What penetrating eye does not everywhere see through the mask? The spectacle is appalling. We live in an atmosphere of hypocrisy throughout. The men believe not in the women, nor the women in the men. A scornful superciliousness rules in literature. The aim of all the *litterateurs* is to find something to make fun of. A lot of churches, sects, &c., the most dismal phantasms I know, usurp the name of religion. Conversation is a mass of badinage. From deceit in the spirit, the mother of all false deeds, the offspring is already incalculable. An acute and candid person, in the Revenue Department in Washington, who is led by the course of his employment to regularly visit the cities, North, South, and West, to investigate frauds, has talked much with

me (1869–70) about his discoveries. The depravity of
the business classes of our country is not less than has
been supposed, but infinitely greater. The whole of the
official services of America, National, State, and Municipal, in all their branches and departments, except the
Judiciary, are steeped, saturated in corruption, bribery,
falsehood, mal-administration; and the Judiciary is
tainted. The great cities reek with respectable as much
as non-respectable robbery and scoundrelism. In fashionable life, flippancy, tepid amours, weak infidelism,
small aims, or no aims at all, only to kill time. In business, (this all-devouring modern word, business,) the one
sole object is, by any means, pecuniary gain. The magician's serpent in the fable ate up all the other serpents; and money-making is our magician's serpent,
remaining to-day sole master of the field. The best
class we show, is but a mob of fashionably-dressed
speculators and vulgarians. True, indeed, behind this
fantastic farce, enacted on the visible stage of society,
solid things and stupendous labors are to be discovered,
existing crudely and going on in the background, to advance and tell themselves in time. Yet the truths are
none the less terrible. I say that our New World Democracy, however great a success in uplifting the masses
out of their sloughs, in materialistic development, products, and in a certain highly-deceptive superficial popular intellectuality, is, so far, an almost complete failure
in its social aspects, in any superb general personal
character, and in really grand religious, moral, literary,
and esthetic results. In vain do we march with unprecedented strides to empire so colossal, outvying the antique, beyond Alexander's, beyond the proudest sway of
Rome. In vain do we annex Texas, California, Alaska,
and reach north for Canada and south for Cuba. It is
as if we were somehow being endowed with a vast and
more and more thoroughly-appointed body, and then
left with little or no soul.

Let me illustrate further, as I write, with current observations, localities, &c. The subject is important, and
will bear repetition. After an absence, I am now (Sep-

tember, 1870,) again in New York City and Brooklyn, on a few weeks' vacation. The splendor, picturesqueness, and oceanic amplitude and rush of these great cities, the unsurpassed situation, rivers and bay, sparkling sea-tides, costly and lofty new buildings, the façades of marble and iron, of original grandeur and elegance of design, with the masses of gay color, the preponderance of white and blue, the flags flying, the endless ships, the tumultuous streets, Broadway, the heavy, low, musical roar, hardly ever intermitted, even at night; the jobbers' houses, the rich shops, the wharves, the great Central Park, and the Brooklyn Park of Hills, (as I wander among them this beautiful fall weather, musing, watching, absorbing,)—the assemblages of the citizens in their groups, conversations, trade, evening amusements, or along the by-quarters—these, I say, and the like of these, completely satisfy my senses of power, fulness, motion, &c., and give me, through such senses and appetites, and through my esthetic conscience, a continued exaltation and absolute fulfilment. Always, and more and more, as I cross the East and North rivers, the ferries, or with the pilots in their pilot-houses, or pass an hour in Wall street, or the gold exchange, I realize, (if we must admit such partialisms,) that not Nature alone is great in her fields of freedom and the open air, in her storms, the shows of night and day, the mountains, forests, seas—but in the artificial, the work of man too is equally great—in this profusion of teeming humanity, in these ingenuities, streets, goods, houses, ships—these seething, hurrying, feverish crowds of men, their complicated business genius, (not least among the geniuses,) and all this mighty, many-threaded wealth and industry concentrated here.

But sternly discarding, shutting our eyes to the glow and grandeur of the general effect, coming down to what is of the only real importance, Personalities, and examining minutely, we question, we ask, Are there, indeed, *Men* here worthy the name? Are there athletes? Are there perfect women, to match the generous material luxuriance? Is there a pervading atmosphere of beautiful manners? Are there crops of fine youths, and majestic old persons? Are there arts worthy Freedom, and a rich people? Is there a great moral and religious civilization—the only justification of a great material one?

Confess that rather to severe eyes, using the moral microscope upon humanity, a sort of dry and flat Sahara appears, these cities, crowded with petty grotesques, malformations, phantoms, playing meaningless antics. Confess that everywhere, in shop, street, church, theatre, bar-room, official chair, are pervading flippancy and vulgarity, low cunning, infidelity—everywhere, the youth puny, impudent, foppish, prematurely ripe—everywhere an abnormal libidinousness, unhealthy forms, male, female, painted, padded, dyed, chignoned, muddy complexions, bad blood, the capacity for good motherhood deceasing or deceased, shallow notions of beauty, with a range of manners, or rather lack of manners, (considering the advantages enjoyed,) probably the meanest to be seen in the world.*

Of all this, and these lamentable conditions, to breathe into them the breath recuperative of sane and heroic life, I say a new founded Literature, not merely to copy and reflect existing surfaces, or pander to what is called taste—not only to amuse, pass away time, celebrate the beautiful, the refined, the past, or exhibit technical,

---

* Of these rapidly-sketched portraitures, hiatuses, the two which seem to me most serious are, for one, the condition, absence, or perhaps the singular abeyance, of moral, conscientious fibre all through American society; and, for another, the appalling depletion of women in their powers of sane athletic maternity, their crowning attribute, and ever making the woman, in loftiest spheres, superior to the man.

I have sometimes thought, indeed, that the sole avenue and means of a reconstructed sociology depended, primarily, on a new birth, elevation, expansion, invigoration of woman, affording, for races to come, (as the conditions that antedate birth are indispensable,) a perfect motherhood. Great, great, indeed far greater than they know, is the sphere of women. But doubtless the question of such new sociology all goes together, includes many varied and complex influences and premises, and the man as well as the woman, and the woman as well as the man.

rhythmic, or grammatical dexterity—but a Literature underlying life, religious, consistent with science, handling the elements and forces with competent power, teaching and training men—and, as perhaps the most precious of its results, achieving the entire redemption of woman out of these incredible holds and webs of silliness, millinery, and every kind of dyspeptic depletion —and thus insuring to The States a strong and sweet Female Race, a race of perfect Mothers—is what is needed.

And now, in the full conception of these facts and points, and all that they infer, pro and con—with yet unshaken faith in the elements of the American masses, the composites, of both sexes, and even considered as individuals—and ever recognizing in them the broadest bases of the best literary and esthetic appreciation —I proceed with my speculations, Vistas.

First, let us see what we can make out of a brief, general, sentimental consideration of political Democracy, and whence it has arisen, with regard to some of its current features, as an aggregate, and as the basic structure of our future literature and authorship. We shall, it is true, quickly and continually find the origin-idea of the singleness of man, individualism, asserting itself, and cropping forth, even from the opposite ideas. But the mass, or lump character, for imperative reasons, is to be ever carefully weighed, borne in mind, and provided for. Only from it, and from its proper regulation and potency, comes the other, comes the chance of Individualism. The two are contradictory, but our task is to reconcile them.*

---

* The question hinted here is one which time only can answer. Must not the virtue of modern Individualism, continually enlarging, usurping all, seriously affect, perhaps keep down entirely, in America, the like of the ancient virtue of Patriotism, the fervid and absorbing love of general country? I have no doubt myself that the two will merge, and will mutually profit and brace each other, and that from them a greater product, a third, will arise. But I feel that at present they and their oppositions form a serious problem and paradox in the United States.

The political history of the past may be summed up as having grown out of what underlies the words Order, Safety, Caste, and especially out of the need of some prompt deciding Authority, and of Cohesion, at all cost. Leaping time, we come to the period within the memory of people now living, when, as from some lair where they had slumbered long, accumulating wrath, sprang up and are yet active, (1790, and on even to the present, 1870,) those noisy eructations, destructive icon-oclasms, a fierce sense of wrongs, and amid which moves the Form, well known in modern history, in the old world, stained with much blood, and marked by savage reactionary clamors and demands. These bear, mostly, as on one enclosing point of need.

For after the rest is said—after the many time-honored and really true things for subordination, experience, rights of property, &c., have been listened to and acquiesced in—after the valuable and well-settled statement of our duties and relations in society is thoroughly conned over and exhausted—it remains to bring forward and modify everything else with the idea of that Something a man is, (last precious consolation of the drudging poor,) standing apart from all else, divine in his own right, and a woman in hers, sole and untouchable by any canons of authority, or any rule derived from precedent, state-safety, the acts of legislatures, or even from what is called religion, modesty, or art.

The radiation of this truth is the key of the most significant doings of our immediately preceding three centuries, and has been the political genesis and life of America. Advancing visibly, it still more advances invisibly. Underneath the fluctuations of the expressions of society, as well as the movements of the politics of the leading nations of the world, we see steadily pressing ahead, and strengthening itself, even in the midst of immense tendencies toward aggregation, this image of completeness in separatism, of individual personal dignity, of a single person, either male or female, characterized in the main, not from extrinsic acquirements or position, but in the pride of himself or herself alone; and, as an eventual conclusion and summing up, (or else the entire scheme of things is aimless, a cheat, a crash,) the simple idea that the last, best dependence is to be upon Humanity itself, and its own inherent, normal, full-grown qualities, without any superstitious support whatever. This idea of perfect individualism it is indeed that deepest tinges and gives character to the idea of the Aggregate. For it is mainly or altogether to serve independent separatism that we favor a strong generalization, consolidation. As it is to give the best vitality and freedom to the rights of the States, (every bit as important as the right of Nationality, the union,) that we insist on the identity of the Union at all hazards.

The purpose of Democracy—supplanting old belief in the necessary absoluteness of established dynastic rulership, temporal, ecclesiastical, and scholastic, as furnishing the only security against chaos, crime, and ignorance—is, through many transmigrations, and amid endless ridicules, arguments, and ostensible failures, to illustrate, at all hazards, this doctrine or theory that man, properly trained in sanest, highest freedom, may and must become a law, and series of laws, unto himself, surrounding and providing for, not only his own personal control, but all his relations to other individuals, and to the State ; and that, while other theories, as in the past histories of nations, have proved wise enough, and indispensable perhaps for their conditions, *this*, as matters now stand in our civilized world, is the only Scheme worth working from, as warranting results like those of Nature's laws, reliable, when once established, to carry on themselves.

The argument of the matter is extensive, and, we admit, by no means all on one side. What we shall offer will be far, far from sufficient. But while leaving unsaid much that should properly even prepare the way for the treatment of this many-sided question of political liberty, equality, or republicanism—leaving the whole history and consideration of the Feudal Plan and its products, embodying Humanity, its politics and civilization, through the retrospect of past time, (which Plan and products, indeed, make up all of the past, and a major part of the present)—Leaving unanswered, at least by any specific and local answer, many a well-wrought argument and instance, and many a conscientious declamatory cry and warning—as, very lately, from an eminent and venerable person abroad *— things, problems, full of doubt, dread, suspense, (not new to me, but old occupiers of many an anxious hour in city's din, or night's silence,) we still may give a page or so, whose drift is opportune. Time alone can finally answer these things. But as a substitute in passing, let us, even if fragmentarily, throw forth a short direct or indirect suggestion of the premises of that other Plan, in the new spirit, under the new forms, started here in our America.

As to the political section of Democracy, which introduces and breaks ground for further and vaster sections, few probably are the minds, even in These Republican States, that fully comprehend the aptness of that phrase, "THE GOVERNMENT OF THE PEOPLE, BY THE PEOPLE, FOR THE PEOPLE," which we inherit from the lips of Abraham Lincoln ; a formula whose verbal shape is homely wit, but whose scope includes both the totality and all minutiæ of the lesson.

The People! Like our huge earth itself, which, to ordinary scansion, is full of vulgar contradictions and offence, Man, viewed in the lump, displeases, and is a constant puzzle and affront to the merely educated classes. The rare, cosmical, artist-mind, lit with the Infinite, alone confronts his manifold and oceanic qualities, but taste, intelligence and culture, (so-called,) have been against the masses, and remain so. There is plenty of glamour about the most damnable crimes and

---

* "SHOOTING NIAGARA."—I was at first roused to much anger and abuse by this Essay from Mr. Carlyle, so insulting to the theory of America—but happening to think afterwards how I had more than once been in the like mood, during which his essay was evidently cast, and seen persons and things in the same light, (indeed some might say there are signs of the same feeling in this book)—I have since read it again, not only as a study, expressing as it does certain judgments from the highest Feudal point of view, but have read it with respect, as coming from an earnest soul, and as contributing certain sharp-cutting metallic grains, which, if not gold or silver, may be good hard, honest iron.

hoggish meannesses, special and general, of the Feudal and dynastic world over there, with its *personnel* of lords and queens and courts; so well-dressed and so handsome. But the People are ungrammatical, untidy, and their sins gaunt and ill-bred.

Literature, strictly considered, has never recognized the People, and, whatever may be said, does not to-day. Speaking generally, the tendencies of literature, as hitherto pursued, have been to make mostly critical and querulous men. It seems as if, so far, there were some natural repugnance between a literary and professional life, and the rude rank spirit of the Democracies. There is, in later literature, a treatment of benevolence, a charity business, rife enough it is true; but I know nothing more rare, even in this country, than a fit scientific estimate and reverent appreciation of the People— of their measureless wealth of latent power and capacity, their vast, artistic contrasts of lights and shades—with, in America, their entire reliability in emergencies, and a certain breadth of historic grandeur, of peace or war, far suspassing all the vaunted samples of book-heroes, or any *haut ton* coteries, in all the records of the world.

The movements of the late Secession war, and their results, to any sense that studies well and comprehends them, show that Popular Democracy, whatever its faults and dangers, practically justifies itself beyond the proudest claims and wildest hopes of its enthusiasts. Probably no future age can know, but I well know, how the gist of this fiercest and most resolute of the world's warlike contentions resided exclusively in the unnamed, unknown rank and file; and how the brunt of its labor of death was, to all essential purposes, Volunteered. The People, of their own choice, fighting, dying for their own idea, insolently attacked by the Secession-Slave-Power, and its very existence imperiled. Descending to detail, entering any of the armies, and mixing with the private soldiers, we see and have seen august spectacles. We have seen the alacrity with which the American-born populace, the peaceablest and most good-natured race in the world, and the most personally independent and intelligent, and the least fitted to submit

to the irksomeness and exasperation of regimental discipline, sprang, at the first tap of the drum, to arms—not
for gain, nor even glory, nor to repel invasion—but for
an emblem, a mere abstraction—for the life, *the safety
of the Flag.* We have seen the unequaled docility and
obedience of these soldiers. We have seen them tried
long and long by hopelessness, mismanagement, and by
defeat ; have seen the incredible slaughter toward or
through which the armies, (as at first Fredericksburg,
and afterward at the Wilderness,) still unhesitating-
ly obeyed orders to advance. We have seen them
in trench, or crouching behind breastwork, or tramp-
ing in deep mud, or amid pouring rain or thick-
falling snow, or under forced marches in hottest summer
(as on the road to get to Gettysburg)—vast suffocating
swarms, divisions, corps, with every single man so grimed
and black with sweat and dust, his own mother would not
have known him—his clothes all dirty, stained and torn,
with sour, accumulated sweat for perfume—many a
comrade, perhaps a brother, sun-struck, staggering out,
dying, by the roadside, of exhaustion—yet the great
bulk bearing steadily on, cheery enough, hollow-bellied
from hunger, but sinewy with unconquerable resolution.

We have seen this race proved by wholesale by
drearier, yet more fearful tests—the wound, the amputation, the shattered face or limb, the slow, hot fever,
long, impatient anchorage in bed, and all the forms of
maiming, operation and disease. Alas ! America have
we seen, though only in her early youth, already to
hospital brought. There have we watched these soldiers, many of them only boys in years—marked their
decorum, their religious nature and fortitude, and their
sweet affection. Wholesale, truly. For at the front, and
through the camps, in countless tents, stood the regimental, brigade and division hospitals ; while everywhere amid the land, in or near cities, rose clusters of
huge, white-washed, crowded, one-story wooden bar-
racks, (Washington City alone, with its suburbs, at
one period, containing in her Army hospitals of this
kind, 50,000 wounded and sick men)—and there ruled
Agony with bitter scourge, yet seldom brought a cry ;

and there stalked Death by day and night along the narrow aisles between the rows of cots, or by the blankets on the ground, and touched lightly many a poor sufferer, often with blessed, welcome touch.

I know not whether I shall be understood, but I realize that it is finally from what I learned personally mixing in such scenes that I am now penning these pages. One night in the gloomiest period of the war, in the Patent Office Hospital in Washington City, as I stood by the bedside of a Pennsylvania soldier, who lay, conscious of quick approaching death, yet perfectly calm, and with noble, spiritual manner, the veteran surgeon, turning aside, said to me, that though he had witnessed many, many deaths of soldiers, and had been a worker at Bull Run, Antietam, Fredericksburg, &c., he had not seen yet the first case of man or boy that met the approach of dissolution with cowardly qualms or terror. My own observation fully bears out the remark.

What have we here, if not, towering above all talk and argument, the plentifully-supplied, last-needed proof of Democracy, in its personalities? Curiously enough, too, the proof on this point comes, I should say, every bit as much from the South, as from the North. Although I have spoken only of the latter, yet I deliberately include all. Grand, common stock! to me the accomplished and convincing growth, prophetic of the future; proof undeniable to sharpest sense, of perfect beauty, tenderness and pluck, that never Feudal lord, nor Greek, nor Roman breed, yet rivaled. Let no tongue ever speak in disparagement of the American races, North or South, to one who has been through the war in the great army hospitals.

Meantime, general Humanity, (for to that we return, as, for our purposes, what it really is, to bear in mind,) has always, in every department, been full of perverse maleficence, and is so yet. In downcast hours the Soul thinks it always will be—but soon recovers from such sickly moods. I, as Democrat, see clearly enough, (as already illustrated,) the crude, defective streaks in all the strata of the common people; the specimens and vast collections of the ignorant, the credulous, the unfit

and uncouth, the incapable, and the very low and poor.
The eminent person just mentioned, sneeringly asks
whether we expect to elevate and improve a Nation's
politics by absorbing such morbid collections and qualities therein. The point is a formidable one, and there
will doubtless always be numbers of solid and reflective
citizens who will never get over it. Our answer is general, and is involved in the scope and letter of this essay.
We believe the ulterior object of political and all other
government, (having, of course, provided for the police,
the safety of life, property, and for the basic statute and
common law, and their administration, always first in
order,) to be, among the rest, not merely to rule, to re-
press disorder, &c., but to develop, to open up to cultivation, to encourage the possibilities of all beneficent
and manly outcroppage, and of that aspiration for independence, and the pride and self-respect latent in all
characters. (Or, if there be exceptions, we cannot, fix-
ing our eyes on them alone, make theirs the rule for all.)

I say the mission of government, henceforth, in civilized lands, is not repression alone, and not authority
alone, not even of law, nor by that favorite standard of
the eminent writer, the rule of the best men, the born
heroes and captains of the race, (as if such ever, or one
time out of a hundred, get into the big places, elective
or dynastic!)—but, higher than the highest arbitrary
rule, to train communities through all their grades, beginning with individuals and ending there again, to rule
themselves.

What Christ appeared for in the moral-spiritual field
for Human-kind, namely, that in respect to the absolute
Soul, there is in the possession of such by each single
individual, something so transcendent, so incapable of
gradations, (like life,) that, to that extent, it places all
beings on a common level, utterly regardless of the distinctions of intellect, virtue, station, or any height or
lowliness whatever—is tallied in like manner, in this
other field, by Democracy's rule that men, the Nation,
as a common aggregate of living identities, affording
in each a separate and complete subject for freedom,
worldly thrift and happiness, and for a fair chance for

growth, and for protection in citizenship, &c., must, to the political extent of the suffrage or vote, if no further, be placed, in each and in the whole, on one broad, primary, universal, common platform.

The purpose is not altogether direct; perhaps it is more indirect. For it is not that Democracy is of exhaustive account, in itself. Perhaps, indeed, it is, (like Nature,) of no account in itself. It is that, as we see, it is the best, perhaps only, fit and full means, formulater, general caller-forth, trainer, for the million, not for grand material personalities only, but for immortal souls. To be a voter with the rest is not so much ; and this, like every institute, will have its imperfections. But to become an enfranchised man, and now, impediments removed, to stand and start without humiliation, and equal with the rest ; to commence, or have the road cleared to commence, the grand experiment of development, whose end, (perhaps requiring several generations,) may be the forming of a full-grown man or woman —that *is* something. To ballast the State is also secured, and in our times is to be secured, in no other way.

We do not, (at any rate I do not,) put it either on the ground that the People, the masses, even the best of them, are, in their latent or exhibited qualities, essentially sensible and good—nor on the ground of their rights ; but that, good or bad, rights or no rights, the Democratic formula is the only safe and preservative one for coming times. We endow the masses with the suffrage for their own sake, no doubt; then, perhaps still more, from another point of view, for community's sake. Leaving the rest to the sentimentalists, we present Freedom as sufficient in its scientific aspects, cold as ice, reasoning, deductive, clear and passionless as crystal.

Democracy too is law, and of the strictest, amplest kind. Many suppose, (and often in its own ranks the error,) that it means a throwing aside of law, and running riot. But, briefly, it is the superior law, not alone that of physical force, the body, which, adding to, it supersedes with that of the spirit. Law is the unshakable order of the universe forever; and the law over all, and law of laws, is the law of successions; that of the superior law, in time, gradually supplanting and over-whelming the inferior one. (While, for myself, I would cheerfully agree—first covenanting that the formative tendencies shall be administered in favor, or, at least not against it, and that this reservation be closely con-strued—that until the individual or community show due signs, or be so minor and fractional as not to en-danger the State, the condition of authoritative tutel-age may continue, and self-government must abide its time.)

—Nor is the esthetic point, always an important one, without fascination for highest aiming souls. The com-mon ambition strains for elevations, to become some privileged exclusive. The master sees greatness and health in being part of the mass. Nothing will do as well as common ground. Would you have in yourself the divine, vast, general law? Then merge yourself in it.

And, topping Democracy, this most alluring record, that it alone can bind, and ever seeks to bind, all na-tions, all men, of however various and distant lands, into a brotherhood, a family. It is the old, yet ever-modern dream of Earth, out of her eldest and her youngest, her fond philosophers and poets. Not that half only, Individualism, which isolates. There is an-other half, which is Adhesiveness or Love, that fuses, ties and aggregates, making the races comrades, and fraternizing all. Both are to be vitalized by Religion, (sole worthiest elevator of man or State,) breathing into the proud, material tissues, the breath of life. For I say at the core of Democracy, finally, is the Religious element. All the Religions, old and new, are there. Nor may the Scheme step forth, clothed in resplendent beauty and command, till these, bearing the best, the latest fruit, the Spiritual, shall fully appear.

A portion of our pages we might indite with refer-ence toward Europe, especially the British part of it, more than our own land, and thus, perhaps not absolutely needed for the home reader. But the whole question hangs together, and fastens and links all peoples. The Liberalist of to-day has this advantage over antique or medieval times, that his doctrine seeks not only to universalize, but to individualize. Then the great word Solidarity has arisen.

I say of all dangers to a Nation, as things exist in our day, there can be no greater one than having certain portions of the people set off from the rest by a line drawn—they not privileged as others, but degraded, humiliated, made of no account. Much quackery teems, of course, even on Democracy's side, yet does not really affect the orbic quality of the matter. To work in, if we may so term it, and justify God, his divine aggregate, the People, (or, the veritable horned and sharp-tailed Devil, *his* aggregate, if there be who convulsively insist upon it,)—this, I say, is what Democracy is for; and this is what our America means, and is doing—may I not say, has done? If not, she means nothing more, and does nothing more, than any other land. And as, by virtue of its kosmical, antiseptic power, Nature's stomach is fully strong enough not only to digest the morbific matter always presented, not to be turned aside, and perhaps, indeed, intuitively gravitating thither—but even to change such contributions into nutriment for highest use and life—so American Democracy's. That is the lesson we, these days, send over to European lands by every western breeze.

And, truly, whatever may be said in the way of abstract argument, for or against the theory of a wider democratizing of institutions in any civilized country, much trouble might well be saved to all European lands by recognizing this palpable fact, (for a palpable fact it is,) that some form of such democratizing is about the only resource now left. *That*, or chronic dissatisfaction continued, mutterings which grow annually louder and louder, till, in due course, and pretty swiftly in most cases, the inevitable crisis, crash, dynastic ruin. Anything worthy to be called statesmanship in the Old World, I should say, among the advanced students,

adepts, or men of any brains, does not debate to-day
whether to hold on, attempting to lean back and mon-
archize, or to look forward and democratize—but *how,*
and in what degree and part, most prudently to democratize. The difficulties of the transfer may be fearful;
perhaps none here in our America can truly know them.
I, for one, fully acknowledge them, and sympathize
deeply. But there is Time, and must be Faith; and
Opportunities, though gradual and slow, will everywhere abroad be born.

There is (turning home again,) a thought, or fact,
I must not forget—subtle and vast, dear to America,
twin-sister of its Democracy—so ligatured indeed to it,
that either's death, if not the other's also, would make
that other live out life, dragging a corpse, a loathsome
horrid tag and burden forever at its feet. What the
idea of Messiah was to the ancient race of Israel,
through storm and calm, through public glory and
their name's humiliation, tenacious, refusing to be argued with, shedding all shafts of ridicule and disbelief,
undestroyed by captivities, battles, deaths—for neither
the scalding blood of war, nor the rotted ichor of peace
could ever wash it out, nor has yet—a great Idea, bed-
ded in Judah's heart—source of the loftiest Poetry the
world yet knows—continuing on the same, though all
else varies—the spinal thread of the incredible romance
of that people's career along five thousand years,—So
runs this thought, this fact, amid our own land's race
and history. It is the thought of Oneness, averaging,
including all; of Identity—the indissoluble sacred
Union of These States.

The eager and often inconsiderate appeals of reformers and revolutionists are indispensable to counter
balance the inertness and fossilism making so large a
part of human institutions. The latter will always take
care of themselves—the danger being that they rapidly
tend to ossify us. The former is to be treated with in-
dulgence, and even respect. As circulation to air, so is
agitation and a plentiful degree of speculative license

to political and moral sanity. Indirectly, but surely, goodness, virtue, law, (of the very best,) follow Freedom. These, to Democracy, are what the keel is to the ship, or saltness to the ocean.

The true gravitation-hold of Liberalism in the United States will be a more universal ownership of property, general homesteads, general comfort—a vast, intertwining reticulation of wealth. As the human frame, or, indeed, any object in this manifold Universe, is best kept together by the simple miracle of its own cohesion, and the necessity, exercise and profit thereof, so a great and varied Nationality, occupying millions of square miles, were firmest held and knit by the principle of the safety and endurance of the aggregate of its middling property owners.

So that, from another point of view, ungracious as it may sound, and a paradox after what we have been saying, Democracy looks with suspicious, ill-satisfied eye upon the very poor, the ignorant, and on those out of business. She asks for men and women with occupations, well-off, owners of houses and acres, and with cash in the bank—and with some cravings for literature, too; and must have them, and hastens to make them. Luckily, the seed is already well-sown, and has taken ineradicable root.*

—Huge and mighty are our Days, our republican lands—and most in their rapid shiftings, their changes, all in the interest of the Cause. As I write this pass-

---

* For fear of mistake, I may as well distinctly announce, as cheerfully included in the model and standard of These Vistas, a practical, stirring, worldly, money-making, even materialistic character. It is undeniable that our farms, stores, offices, dry-goods, coal and groceries, enginery, cash-accounts, trades, earnings, markets, &c., should be attended to in earnest, and actively pursued, just as if they had a real and permanent existence. I perceive clearly that the extreme business energy, and this almost maniacal appetite for wealth prevalent in the United States, are vital parts of amelioration and progress, and perhaps indispensably needed to prepare the very results I demand. My theory includes riches, and the getting of riches, and the amplest products, power, activity, inventions, movements, &c. Upon these, as upon substrata, I raise the edifice designed in These Vistas.

age, (November, 1868,) the din of disputation rages
around me. Acrid the temper of the parties, vital the
pending questions. Congress convenes ; the President
sends his Message ; Reconstruction is still in abeyance ;
the nominations and the contest for the twenty-first
Presidentiad draw close, with loudest threat and bustle.
Of these, and all the like of these, the eventuations I
know not ; but well I know that behind them, and whatever their eventuations, the really vital things remain
safe and certain, and all the needed work goes on.
Time, with soon or later superciliousness, disposes of
Presidents, Congressmen, party platforms, and such.
Anon, it clears the stage of each and any mortal shred
that thinks itself so potent to its day ; and at and after
which, (with precious, golden exceptions once or twice
in a century,) all that relates to sir potency is flung to
moulder in a burial-vault, and no one bothers himself
the least bit about it afterward. But the People ever
remains, tendencies continue, and all the idiocratic
transfers in unbroken chain go on. In a few years the
dominion-heart of America will be far inland, toward
the West. Our future National Capitol may not be
where the present one is. It is possible, nay likely, that
in less than fifty years, it will migrate a thousand or two
miles, will be re-founded, and every thing belonging to
it made on a different plan, original, far more superb.
The main social, political spine-character of The States
will probably run along the Ohio, Missouri and Mississippi Rivers, and west and north of them, including
Canada. Those regions, with the group of powerful
brothers toward the Pacific, (destined to the mastership
of that sea and its countless Paradises of islands,) will
compact and settle the traits of America, with all the
old retained, but more expanded, grafted on newer,
hardier, purely native stock. A giant growth, compo-
site from the rest, getting their contribution, absorbing
it, to make it more illustrious. From the North, Intellect, the sun of things—also the idea of unswayable
Justice, anchor amid the last, the wildest tempests.
From the South, the living Soul, the animus of good
and bad, haughtily admitting no demonstration but its

own. While from the West itself comes solid Personality, with blood and brawn, and the deep quality of all-accepting fusion.

Political Democracy, as it exists and practically works in America, with all its threatening evils, supplies a training-school for making grand young men. It is life's gymnasium, not of good only, but of all. We try often, though we fall back often. A brave delight, fit for freedom's athletes, fills these arenas, and fully satisfies, out of the action in them, irrespective of success. Whatever we do not attain, we at any rate attain the experiences of the fight, the hardening of the strong campaign, and throb with currents of attempt at least. Time is ample. Let the victors come after us. Not for nothing does evil play its part among men. Judging from the main portions of the history of the world, so far, justice is always in jeopardy, peace walks amid hourly pitfalls, and of slavery, misery, meanness, the craft of tyrants and the credulity of the populace, in some of their protean forms, no voice can at any time say, They are not. The clouds break a little, and the sun shines out—but soon and certain the lowering darkness falls again, as if to last forever. Yet is there an immortal courage and prophecy in every sane soul that cannot, must not, under any circumstances, capitulate. *Vive*, the attack—the perennial assault! *Vive*, the unpopular cause—the spirit that audaciously aims—the never-abandoned efforts, pursued the same amid opposing proofs and precedents.

—Once, before the war, (Alas! I dare not say how many times the mood has come!) I, too, was filled with doubt and gloom. A foreigner, an acute and good man, had impressively said to me, that day—putting in form, indeed, my own observations : I have traveled much in the United States, and watched their politicians, and listened to the speeches of the candidates, and read the journals, and gone into the public houses, and heard the unguarded talk of men. And I have found your vaunted America honey-combed from top to toe with infidelism, even to itself and its own programme. I have marked the brazen hell-faces of secession and slavery gazing defiantly from all the windows and door-ways. I have everywhere found, primarily, thieves and scalliwags arranging the nominations to offices, and sometimes filling the offices themselves. I have found the North just as full of bad stuff as the South. Of the holders of public office in the Nation, or in the States, or their municipalities, I have found that not one in a hundred has been chosen by any spontaneous selection of the outsiders, the people, but all have been nominated and put through by little or large caucuses of the politicians, and have got in by corrupt rings and elec-tioneering, not capacity or desert. I have noticed how the millions of sturdy farmers and mechanics are thus the helpless supple-jacks of comparatively few politi-cians. And I have noticed more and more, the alarm-ing spectacle of parties usurping the Government, and openly and shamelessly wielding it for party purposes.

Sad, serious, deep truths. Yet are there other, still deeper, amply confronting, dominating truths. Over those politicians and great and little rings, and over all their insolence and wiles, and over the powerfulest par-ties, looms a Power, too sluggish may-be, but ever hold-ing decisions and decrees in hand, ready, with stern process, to execute them as soon as plainly needed, and at times, indeed, summarily crushing to atoms the mightiest parties, even in the hour of their pride.

In saner hours far different are the amounts of these things from what, at first sight, they appear. Though it is no doubt important who is elected President or Governor, Mayor or Legislator, (and full of dismay when incompetent or vile ones get elected, as they sometimes do,) there are other, quieter contingencies, infinitely more important. Shams, &c., will always be the show, like ocean's scum; enough, if waters deep and clear make up the rest. Enough, that while the piled embroidered shoddy gaud and fraud spreads to the superficial eye, the hidden warp and weft are gen-uine, and will wear forever. Enough, in short, that the race, the land which could raise such as the late Rebel-lion, could also put it down.

The average man of a land at last only is important. He, in These States, remains immortal owner and boss, deriving good uses, somehow, out of any sort of servant in office, even the basest; because, (certain universal requisites, and their settled regularity and protection, being first secured,) a Nation like ours, in a sort of geological formation state, trying continually new experiments, choosing new delegations, is not served by the best men only, but sometimes more by those that provoke it—by the combats they arouse. Thus national rage, fury, discussion, &c., better than content. Thus, also, the warning signals, invaluable for after times.

What is more dramatic than the spectacle we have seen repeated, and doubtless long shall see—the popular judgment taking the successful candidates on trial in the offices—standing off, as it were, and observing them and their doings for a while, and always giving, finally, the fit, exactly due reward?

I think, after all, the sublimest part of political history, and its culmination, is currently issuing from the American people. I know nothing grander, better exercise, better digestion, more positive proof of the past, the triumphant result of faith in humankind, than a well-contested American national election.

Then still the thought returns, (like the thread-passage in overtures,) giving the key and echo to these pages. When I pass to and fro, different latitudes, different seasons, beholding the crowds of the great cities, New York, Boston, Philadelphia, Cincinnati, Chicago, St. Louis, San Francisco, New Orleans, Baltimore—when I mix with these interminable swarms of alert, turbulent, good-natured, independent citizens, mechanics, clerks, young persons—at the idea of this mass of men, so fresh and free, so loving and so proud, a singular awe falls upon me. I feel, with dejection and amazement, that among our geniuses and talented writers or speakers, few or none have yet really spoken to this people, or created a single image-making work that could be called for them—or absorbed the central spirit and the idiosyncrasies which are theirs, and which, thus, in highest ranges, so far remain entirely uncelebrated, unexpressed.

Dominion strong is the body's ; dominion stronger is the mind's. What has filled, and fills to-day our intellect, our fancy, furnishing the standards therein, is yet foreign. The great poems, Shakespeare included, are poisonous to the idea of the pride and dignity of the common people, the life-blood of Democracy. The models of our literature, as we get it from other lands, ultramarine, have had their birth in courts, and basked and grown in castle sunshine ; all smells of princes' favors. Of workers of a certain sort, we have, indeed, plenty, contributing after their kind ; many elegant, many learned, all complacent. But, touched by the National test, or tried by the standards of Democratic personality, they wither to ashes. I say I have not seen a single writer, artist, lecturer, or what not, that has confronted the voiceless but ever erect and active, pervading, underlying will and typic Aspiration of the land, in a spirit kindred to itself. Do you call those genteel little creatures American poets ? Do you term that perpetual, pistareen, paste-pot work, American art, American drama, taste, verse ? I think I hear, echoed as from some mountain-top afar in the West, the scornful laugh of the Genius of These States.

—Democracy, in silence, biding its time, ponders its own ideals, not of Literature and Art only—not of men only, but of women. The idea of the women of America, (extricated from this daze, this fossil and unhealthy air which hangs about the word Lady,) developed, raised to become the robust equals, workers, and, it may be, even practical and political deciders with the men— greater than man, we may admit, through their divine maternity, always their towering, emblematical attribute—but great, at any rate, as man, in all departments ; or, rather, capable of being so, soon as they realize it, and can bring themselves to give up toys and fictions, and launch forth, as men do, amid real, independent, stormy life.

—Then, as toward our thought's finale, (and, in that,

overarching the true scholar's lesson,) we have to say there can be no complete or epical presentation of Democracy in the aggregate, or any thing like it, at this day, because its doctrines will only be effectually incarnated in any one branch, when, in all, their spirit is at the root and centre. Far, far, indeed, stretch, in distance, our vistas! How much is still to be disentangled, freed! How long it takes to make this world see that it is, in itself, the final authority and reliance!

Did you, too, O friend, suppose Democracy was only for elections, for politics, and for a party name? I say Democracy is only of use there that it may pass on and come to its flower and fruits in manners, in the highest forms of interaction between men, and their beliefs—in Religion, Literature, colleges, and schools—Democracy in all public and private life, and in the Army and Navy.* I have intimated that, as a paramount scheme, it has yet few or no full realizers and believers. I do not see, either, that it owes any serious thanks to noted propagandists or champions, or has been essentially helped, though often harmed, by them. It has been and is carried on by all the moral forces, and by trade, finance, machinery, intercommunications, and, in fact, by all the developments of history, and can no more be stopped than the tides, or the earth in its orbit. Doubtless, also, it resides, crude and latent, well down in the hearts of the fair average of the American-born people, mainly in the agricultural regions. But it is not yet, there or anywhere, the fully-received, the fervid, the absolute faith.

I submit, therefore, that the fruition of Democracy, on aught like a grand scale, resides altogether in the future. As, under any profound and comprehensive view of the gorgeous-composite Feudal world, we see

---

* The whole present system of the officering and *personnel* of the Army and Navy of These States, and the spirit and letter of their trebly-aristocratic rules and regulations, is a monstrous exotic, a nuisance and revolt, and belong here just as much as orders of nobility, or the Pope's council of Cardinals. I say if the present theory of our Army and Navy is sensible and true, then the rest of America is an unmitigated fraud.

in it, through the long ages and cycles of ages, the results of a deep, integral, human and divine principle, or
fountain, from which issued laws, ecclesia, manners, institutes, costumes, personalities, poems, (hitherto unequaled,) faithfully partaking of their source, and indeed only arising either to betoken it, or to furnish
parts of that varied-flowing display, whose centre was
one and absolute—so, long ages hence, shall the due
historian or critic make at least an equal retrospect, an
equal History for the Democratic principle. It, too,
must be adorned, credited with its results—then, when
it, with imperial power, through amplest time, has domi-
nated mankind—has been the source and test of all the
moral, esthetic, social, political, and religious expressions and institutes of the civilized world—has begotten
them in spirit and in form, and carried them to its own
unprecedented heights—has had, (it is possible,) monas-
tics and ascetics, more numerous, more devout than the
monks and priests of all previous creeds—has swayed
the ages with a breadth and rectitude tallying Nature's
own—has fashioned, systematized, and triumphantly finished and carried out, in its own interest, and with unparalleled success, a New Earth and a New Man.

—Thus we presume to write, as it were, upon things
that exist not, and travel by maps yet unmade, and a
blank. But the throes of birth are upon us; and we
have something of this advantage in seasons of strong
formations, doubts, suspense—for then the afflatus of
such themes haply may fall upon us, more or less; and
then, hot from surrounding war and revolution, our
speech, though without polished coherence, and a failure by the standard called criticism, comes forth, real
at least, as the lightnings.

And may-be we, these days, have, too, our own reward—(for there are yet some, in all lands, worthy to
be so encouraged.) Though not for us the joy of entering at the last the conquered city—nor ours the
chance ever to see with our own eyes the peerless
power and splendid *eclat* of the Democratic principle,
arrived at meridian, filling the world with effulgence
and majesty far beyond those of past history's kings,

or all dynastic sway—there is yet, to whoever is eligible among us, the prophetic vision, the joy of being tossed in the brave turmoil of these times—the promulgation and the path, obedient, lowly reverent to the voice, the gesture of the god, or holy ghost, which others see not, hear not—with the proud consciousness that amid whatever clouds, seductions, or heart-wearying postponements, we have never deserted, never despaired, never abandoned the Faith.

So much contributed, to be conned well, to help prepare and brace our edifice, our plann'd Idea—we still proceed to give it in another of its aspects—perhaps the main, the high façade of all. For to Democracy, the leveler, the unyielding principle of the average, is surely joined another principle, equally unyielding, closely tracking the first, indispensable to it, opposite, (as the sexes are opposite,) and whose existence, confronting and ever modifying the other, often clashing, paradoxical, yet neither of highest avail without the other, plainly supplies to these grand cosmic politics of ours, and to the launched forth mortal dangers of Republicanism, to-day or any day, the counterpart and offset, whereby Nature restrains the deadly original relentlessness of all her first-class laws. This second principle is Individuality, the pride and centripetal isolation of a human being in himself,—Identity—Personalism. Whatever the name, its acceptance and thorough infusion through the organizations of political commonalty now shooting Aurora-like about the world, are of utmost importance, as the principle itself is needed for very life's sake. It forms, in a sort, or is to form, the compensating balance-wheel of the successful working machinery of aggregate America.

—And, if we think of it, what does civilization itself rest upon—and what object has it, with its religions, arts, schools, &c., but rich, luxuriant, varied Personalism? To that, all bends; and it is because toward such result Democracy alone, on anything like Nature's scale, breaks up the limitless fallows of humankind, and plants

the seed, and gives fair play, that its claims now precede
the rest.

The Literature, Songs, Esthetics, &c., of a country
are of importance principally because they furnish the
materials and suggestions of Personality for the women
and men of that country, and enforce them in a thousand effective ways.*

As the topmost claim of a strong consolidating of the
Nationality of These States, is, that only by such powerful compaction can the separate States secure that full
and free swing within their spheres, which is becoming
to them, each after its kind, so will Individuality, with
unimpeded branchings, flourish best under imperial Republican forms.

—Assuming Democracy to be at present in its embryo

---

* After the rest is satiated, all interest culminates in the field of
Persons, and never flags there. Accordingly in this field have
the great Poets and Literatuses signally toiled. They too, in all
ages, all lands, have been creators, fashioning, making types of
men and women, as Adam and Eve are made in the divine fable.
Behold, shaped, bred by Orientalism, Feudalism, through their
long growth and culmination, and breeding back in return,
(When shall we have an equal series, typical of Democracy ?)—
Behold, commencing in primal Asia, (apparently formulated, in
what beginning we know, in the gods of the mythologies, and
coming down thence,) a few samples out of the countless product,
bequeathed to the moderns, bequeathed to America as studies.
For the men, Yudishtura, Rama, Arjuna, Solomon, most of the
Old and New Testament characters ; Achilles, Ulysses, Theseus,
Prometheus, Hercules, Æneas, St. John, Plutarch's heroes; the
Merlin of Celtic bards, the Cid, Arthur and his knights, Siegfried
and Hagen in the Niebelungen; Roland and Oliver ; Roustam in
the Shah-Nehmah ; and so on to Milton's Satan, Cervantes' Don
Quixote, Shakespeare's Hamlet, Richard II., Lear, Marc Antony,
&c., and the modern Faust. These, I say, are models, combined,
adjusted to other standards than America's, but of priceless value
to her and hers.

Among women, the goddesses of the Egyptian, Indian and
Greek mythologies, certain Bible characters, especially the Holy
Mother; Cleopatra, Penelope; the portraits of Brunhelde and
Chriemhilde in the Niebelungen ; Oriana, Una, &c. ; the modern
Consuelo, Walter Scott's Jeanie and Effie Deans, &c., &c. (Woman,
portrayed or outlined at her best, or as perfect human Mother,
does not yet, it seems to me, fully appear in Literature.)

condition, and that the only large and satisfactory justification of it resides in the future, mainly through the copious production of perfect characters among the people, and through the advent of a sane and pervading Religiousness, it is with regard to the atmosphere and spaciousness fit for such characters, and of certain nutriment and cartoon-draftings proper for them, and indicating them, for New World purposes, that I continue the present statement—an exploration, as of new ground, wherein, like other primitive surveyors, I must do the best I can, leaving it to those who come after me to do much better. The service, in fact, if any, must be to merely break a sort of first path or track, no matter how rude and ungeometrical.

We have frequently printed the word Democracy. Yet I cannot too often repeat that it is a word the real gist of which still sleeps, quite unawakened, notwithstanding the resonance and the many angry tempests, out of which its syllables have come, from pen or tongue. It is a great word, whose history, I suppose, remains unwritten, because that history has yet to be enacted. It is, in some sort, younger brother of another great and often-used word, Nature, whose history also waits unwritten.

As I perceive, the tendencies of our day, in The States, (and I entirely respect them,) are toward those vast and sweeping movements, influences, moral and physical, of humanity, now and always current over the planet, on the scale of the impulses of the elements. Then it is also good to reduce the whole matter to the consideration of a single self, a man, a woman, on permanent grounds. Even for the treatment of the universal, in politics, metaphysics, or anything, sooner or later we come down to one single, solitary Soul.

There is, in sanest hours, a consciousness, a thought that rises, independent, lifted out from all else, calm, like the stars, shining eternal. This is the thought of Identity—yours for you, whoever you are, as mine for me. Miracle of miracles, beyond statement, most spiritual and vaguest of earth's dreams, yet hardest basic fact, and only entrance to all facts. In such devout hours, in the midst of the significant wonders of heaven and earth, (significant only because of the Me in the centre,) creeds, conventions, fall away and become of no account before this simple idea. Under the luminousness of real vision, it alone takes possession, takes value. Like the shadowy dwarf in the fable, once liberated and looked upon, it expands over the whole earth, and spreads to the roof of heaven.

The quality of BEING, in the object's self, according to its own central idea and purpose, and of growing therefrom and thereto—not criticism by other standards, and adjustments thereto—is the lesson of Nature. True, the full man wisely gathers, culls, absorbs; but if, engaged disproportionately in that, he slights or overlays the precious idiocrasy and special nativity and intention that he is, the man's self, the main thing, is a failure, however wide his general cultivation. Thus, in our times, refinement and delicatesse are not only attended to sufficiently, but threaten to eat us up, like a cancer. Already, the Democratic genius watches, ill-pleased, these tendencies. Provision for a little healthy rudeness, savage virtue, justification of what one has in one's self, whatever it is, is demanded. Negative qualities, even deficiencies, would be a relief. Singleness and normal simplicity, and separation, amid this more and more complex, more and more artificialized, state of society—how pensively we yearn for them! how we would welcome their return!

In some such direction, then—at any rate enough to preserve the balance—we feel called upon to throw what weight we can, not for absolute reasons, but current ones. To prune, gather, trim, conform, and ever cram and stuff, is the pressure of our days. While aware that much can be said even in behalf of all this, we perceive that we have not now to consider the question of what is demanded to serve a half-starved and barbarous nation, or set of nations, but what is most applicable, most pertinent, for numerous congeries of conventional, over-corpulent societies already becoming stifled and rotten with flatulent, infidelistic literature, and polite conformity and art.

In addition to established sciences, we suggest a
science as it were of healthy average Personalism, on
original-universal grounds, the object of which should
be to raise up and supply through The States a copious
race of superb American men and women, cheerful, religious, ahead of any yet known.

America, leaving out her politics, has yet morally
originated nothing. She seems singularly unaware that
the models of persons, books, manners, &c., appropriate
for former conditions and for European lands, are but
exiles and exotics here. No current of her life, as shown
on the surfaces of what is authoritatively called her Society, accepts or runs into moral, social, or esthetic Democracy; but all the currents set squarely against it.
Never, in the Old World, was thoroughly upholstered
Exterior Appearance and show, mental and other, built
entirely on the idea of caste, and on the sufficiency of
mere outside Acquisition—never were Glibness, verbal
Intellect, more the test, the emulation—more loftily
elevated as head and sample—than they are on the
surface of our Republican States this day. The writers
of a time hint the mottoes of its gods. The word of
the modern, say these voices, is the word Culture.

We find ourselves abruptly in close quarters with the
enemy. This word Culture, or what it has come to represent, involves, by contrast, our whole theme, and has
been, indeed, the spur, urging us to engagement. Certain questions arise.

As now taught, accepted and carried out, are not the
processes of Culture rapidly creating a class of super-
cilious infidels, who believe in nothing? Shall a man
lose himself in countless masses of adjustments, and be
so shaped with reference to this, that, and the other,
that the simply good and healthy and brave parts of
him are reduced and clipped away, like the bordering
of box in a garden? You can cultivate corn and roses
and orchards—but who shall cultivate the primæval
forests, the mountain peaks, the ocean, and the tum-
bling gorgeousness of the clouds? Lastly—Is the
readily-given reply that Culture only seeks to help,

systematize, and put in attitude, the elements of fertility and power, a conclusive reply?

I do not so much object to the name, or word, but I should certainly insist, for the purposes of These States, on a radical change of category, in the distribution of precedence. I should demand a programme of Culture, drawn out, not for a single class alone, or for the parlors or lecture-rooms, but with an eye to practical life, the West, the working-men, the facts of farms and jackplanes and engineers, and of the broad range of the women also of the middle and working strata, and with reference to the perfect equality of women, and of a grand and powerful motherhood. I should demand of this programme or theory a scope generous enough to include the widest human area. It must have for its spinal meaning the formation of a typical Personality of character, eligible to the uses of the high average of men—and *not* restricted by conditions ineligible to the masses.

The best culture will always be that of the manly and courageous instincts, and loving perceptions, and of self-respect—aiming to form, over this continent, an Idiocrasy of Universalism, which, true child of America, will bring joy to its mother, returning to her in her own spirit, recruiting myriads of men, able, natural, perceptive, tolerant, devout, real men, alive and full, believers in her, America, and with some definite instinct why and for what she has arisen, most vast, most formidable of historic births, and is, now and here, with wonderful step, journeying through Time.

The problem, as it seems to me, presented to the New World, is, under permanent law and order, and after preserving cohesion, (ensemble-Individuality,) at all hazards, to vitalize man's free play of special Personalism, recognizing in it something that calls ever more to be considered, fed, and adopted as the substratum for the best that belongs to us, (government indeed is for it,) including the new esthetics of our future.

To formulate beyond this present vagueness—to help line and put before us, the species, or a specimen of the species, of the Democratic ethnology of the future, is a work toward which the Genius of our land, with peculiar encouragement, invites her well-wishers. Already, certain limnings, more or less grotesque, more or less fading and watery, have appeared. We too, (repressing doubts and qualms,) will try our hand.

Attempting then, however crudely, a basic model or portrait of Personality, for general use for the manliness of The States, (and doubtless that is most useful which is most simple, comprehensive for all, and toned low enough,) we should prepare the canvas well beforehand. Parentage must consider itself in advance. (Will the time hasten when fatherhood and motherhood shall become a science—and the noblest science?) To our model a clear-blooded, strong-fibred physique, is indispensable; the questions of food, drink, air, exercise, assimilation, digestion, can never be intermitted. Out of these we descry a well-begotten Selfhood—in youth, fresh, ardent, emotional, aspiring, full of adventure; at maturity, brave, perceptive, under control, neither too talkative nor too reticent, neither flippant nor sombre; of the bodily figure, the movements easy, the complexion showing the best blood, somewhat flushed, breast expanded, an erect attitude, a voice whose sound outvies music, eyes of calm and steady gaze, yet capable also of flashing—and a general presence that holds its own in the company of the highest. For it is native Personality, and that alone, that endows a man to stand before Presidents or Generals, or in any distinguished collection, with *aplomb;* and *not* Culture, or any knowledge or intellect whatever.

With regard to the mental-educational part of our model, enlargement of intellect, stores of cephalic knowledge, &c., the concentration thitherward of all the customs of our age, especially in America, is so overweening, and provides so fully for that part, that, important and necessary as it is, it really needs nothing from us here—except, indeed, a phrase of warning and restraint.

Manners, costumes, too, though important, we need not dwell upon here. Like beauty, grace of motion,

&c., they are results. Causes, original things, being attended to, the right manners unerringly follow. Much is said, among artists, of the grand style, as if it were a thing by itself. When a man, artist or whoever, has health, pride, acuteness, noble aspirations, he has the motive-elements of the grandest style. The rest is but manipulation, (yet that is no small matter.)

—Leaving still unspecified several sterling parts of any model fit for the future Personality of America, I must not fail, again and ever, to pronounce myself on one, probably the least attended to in modern times—a hiatus, indeed, threatening its gloomiest consequences after us. I mean the simple, unsophisticated Conscience, the primary moral element. If I were asked to specify in what quarter lie the grounds of darkest dread, respecting the America of our hopes, I should have to point to this particular. I should demand the invariable application to Individuality, this day, and any day, of that old, ever-true plumb-rule of persons, eras, nations. Our triumphant modern Civilizee, with his all-schooling and his wondrous appliances, will still show himself but an amputation while this deficiency remains.

Beyond, (assuming a more hopeful tone,) the vertebration of the manly and womanly Personalism of our Western World, can only be, and is, indeed, to be, (I hope,) its all penetrating Religiousness. The architecture of Individuality will ever prove various, with countless different combinations ; but here they rise as into common pinnacles, some higher, some less high, only all pointing upward.

Indeed, the ripeness of Religion is doubtless to be looked for in this field of Individuality, and is a result that no organization or church can ever achieve. As history is poorly retained by what the technists call history, and is not given out from their pages, except the learner has in himself the sense of the well-wrapt, never yet written, perhaps impossible to be written, history— so Religion, although casually arrested, and, after a fashion, preserved in the churches and creeds, does not depend at all upon them, but is a part of the identified

Soul, which, when greatest, knows not Bibles in the old way, but in new ways—the identified Soul, which can really confront Religion when it extricates itself entirely from the churches, and not before.

Personalism fuses this, and favors it. I should say, indeed, that only in the perfect uncontamination and solitariness of Individuality may the spirituality of Religion positively come forth at all. Only here, and on such terms, the meditation, the devout ecstasy, the soaring flight. Only here, communion with the mysteries, the eternal problems, Whence? whither? Alone, and identity, and the mood—and the Soul emerges, and all statements, churches, sermons, melt away like vapors. Alone, and silent thought, and awe, and aspiration—and then the interior consciousness, like a hitherto unseen inscription, in magic ink, beams out its wondrous lines to the sense. Bibles may convey, and priests expound, but it is exclusively for the noiseless operation of one's isolated Self, to enter the pure ether of veneration, reach the divine levels, and commune with the unutterable.

To practically enter into Politics is an important part of American personalism. To every young man, North and South, earnestly studying these things, I should here, as an offset to what I have said in former pages, now also say, that may-be to views of very largest scope, after all, perhaps the political, (and perhaps literary and sociological,) America goes best about its development its own way—sometimes, to temporary sight, appalling enough. It is the fashion among dillettants and fops to decry the whole formulation and *personnel* of the active politics of America, as beyond redemption, and to be carefully kept away from. See you that you do not fall into this error. America, it may be, is doing very well, upon the whole, notwithstanding these antics of the parties and their leaders, these half-brained nominees, and the many ignorant ballots, and many elected failures and blatherers. It is the dillettants, and all who shirk their duty, who are not doing well. As for you, I advise you to enter more strongly yet into politics. I advise every young man to do so. Always inform yourself; always do the best you can; always vote. Disengage yourself from parties. They have been useful, and to some extent remain so; but the floating, uncommitted electors, farmers, clerks, mechanics, the masters of parties—watching aloof, inclining victory this side or that side—such are the ones most needed, present and future. For America, if eligible at all to downfall and ruin, is eligible within herself, not without; for I see clearly that the combined foreign world could not beat her down. But these savage, wolfish parties alarm me. Owning no law but their own will, more and more combative, less and less tolerant of the idea of ensemble and of equal brotherhood, the perfect equality of the States, the ever-overarching American ideas, it behooves you to convey yourself implicitly to no party, nor submit blindly to their dictators, but steadily hold yourself judge and master over all of them.

—So much, (hastily tossed together, and leaving far more unsaid,) for an ideal, or intimations of an ideal, toward American manhood. But the other sex, in our land, requires at least a basis of suggestion.

I have seen a young American woman, one of a large family of daughters, who, some years since, migrated from her meagre country home to one of the northern cities, to gain her own support. She soon became an expert seamstress, but finding the employment too confining for her health and comfort, she went boldly to work, for others, to house-keep, cook, clean, &c. After trying several places, she fell upon one where she was suited. She has told me that she finds nothing degrading in her position; it is not inconsistent with personal dignity, self-respect, and the respect of others. She confers benefits and receives them. She has good health; her presence itself is healthy and bracing; her character is unstained; she has made herself understood, and preserves her independence, and has been able to help her parents and educate and get places for her sisters; and her course of life is not without opportunities for mental improvement, and of much quiet, uncosting happiness and love.

I have seen another woman who, from taste and necessity conjoined, has gone into practical affairs, carries on a mechanical business, partly works at it herself, dashes out more and more into real hardy life, is not abashed by the coarseness of the contact, knows how to be firm and silent at the same time, holds her own with unvarying coolness and decorum, and will compare, any day, with superior carpenters, farmers, and even boatmen and drivers. For all that, she has not lost the charm of the womanly nature, but preserves and bears it fully, though through such rugged presentation.

Then there is the wife of a mechanic, mother of two children, a woman of merely passable English education, but of fine wit, with all her sex's grace and intuitions, who exhibits, indeed, such a noble female Personality, that I am fain to record it here. Never abnegating her own proper independence, but always genially preserving it, and what belongs to it—cooking, washing, child-nursing, house-tending, she beams sunshine out of all these duties, and makes them illustrious. Physiologically sweet and sound, loving work, practical, she yet knows that there are intervals, however few, devoted to recreation, music, leisure, hospitality—and affords such intervals. Whatever she does, and wherever she is, that charm, that indescribable perfume of genuine womanhood, attends her, goes with her, exhales from her, which belongs of right to all the sex, and is, or ought to be, the invariable atmosphere and common aureola of old as well as young.

My mother has described to me a resplendent person, down on Long Island, whom she knew years ago, in early days. She was known by the name of the Peacemaker. She was well toward eighty years old, of happy and sunny temperament, had always lived on a farm, was very neighborly, sensible and discreet, an invariable and welcomed favorite, especially with young married women. She had numerous children and grandchildren. She was uneducated, but possessed a native dignity. She had come to be a tacitly agreed upon domestic regulator, judge, settler of difficulties, shepherdess, and reconciler in the land. She was a sight to draw near and look upon, with her large figure, her profuse snow-white hair, dark eyes, clear complexion, sweet breath, and peculiar personal magnetism.

The foregoing portraits, I admit, are frightfully out of line from these imported models of womanly Personality—the stock feminine characters of the current novelists, or of the foreign court poems, (Ophelias, Enids, Princesses, or Ladies of one thing or another,) which fill the envying dreams of so many poor girls, and are accepted by our young men, too, as supreme ideals of feminine excellence to be sought after. But I present mine just for a change.

Then there are mutterings, (we will not now stop to heed them here, but they must be heeded,) of something more revolutionary. The day is coming when the deep questions of woman's entrance amid the arenas of practical life, politics, trades, &c., will not only be argued all around us, but may be put to decision, and real experiment.

—Of course, in These States, for both man and woman, we must entirely recast the types of highest Personality from what the Oriental, Feudal, Ecclesiastical worlds bequeath us, and which yet fully possess the imaginative and esthetic fields of the United States, pictorial and melodramatic, not without use as studies, but making sad work, and forming a strange anachronism upon the scenes and exigencies around us.

Of course, the old, undying elements remain. The task is, to successfully adjust them to new combinations, our own days. Nor is this so incredible. I can conceive a community, to-day and here, in which, on a sufficient scale, the perfect Personalities, without noise, meet; say in some pleasant Western settlement or town, where a couple of hundred best men and women, of ordinary worldly status, have by luck been drawn together, with nothing extra of genius or wealth, but virtuous, chaste, industrious, cheerful, resolute, friendly,

and devout. I can conceive such a community organized in running order, powers judiciously delegated,
farming, building, trade, courts, mails, schools, elections, all attended to ; and then the rest of life, the
main thing, freely branching and blossoming in each
individual, and bearing golden fruit. I can see there,
in every young and old man, after his kind, and in every
woman after hers, a true Personality, developed, exercised proportionately in body, mind, and spirit. I can
imagine this case as one not necessarily rare or difficult,
but in buoyant accordance with the municipal and general requirements of our times. And I can realize in
it the culmination of something better than any stereo-
typed *eclat* of history or poems. Perhaps, unsung, un-
dramatized, unput in essays or biographies—perhaps
even some such community already exists, in Ohio, Illi-
nois, Missouri, or somewhere, practically fulfilling itself,
and thus outvying, in cheapest vulgar life, all that has
been hitherto shown in best ideal pictures.

In short, and to sum up, America, betaking herself
to formative action, (as it is about time for more solid
achievement and less windy promise,) must, for her
purposes, cease to recognize a theory of character
grown of Feudal aristocracies, or formed by merely
esthetic or literary standards, or from any ultramarine,
full-dress formulas of culture, polish, caste, &c., and
must sternly promulgate her own new standard, yet
old enough, and accepting the old, the perennial, elements, and combining them into groups, unities, appropriate to the modern, the democratic, the West, and to
the practical occasions and needs of our own cities, and
of the agricultural regions. Ever the most precious in
the common. Ever the fresh breeze of field, or hill, or
lake, is more than any palpitation of fans, though of
ivory, and redolent with perfume ; and the air is more
than the costliest perfumes.

And now, for fear of mistake, we may not intermit to
beg our absolution from all that genuinely is, or goes
along with, even Culture. Pardon us, venerable shade !
if we have seemed to speak lightly of your office. The
whole civilization of the earth, we know, is yours, with

all the glory and the light thereof. It is, indeed, in your own spirit, and seeking to tally the loftiest teachings of it, that we aim these poor utterances. For you, too, mighty minister! know that there is something greater than you, namely, the fresh, eternal qualities of Being. From them, and by them, as you, at your best, we, too, after our fashion, when art and conventions fail, evoke the last, the needed help, to vitalize our country and our days.

Thus we pronounce not so much against the principle of Culture; we only supervise it, and promulge along with it, as deep, perhaps a deeper, principle. As we have shown, the New World, including in itself the all-leveling aggregate of Democracy, we show it also including the all-varied, all-permitting, all-free theorem of Individuality, and erecting therefor a lofty and hitherto unoccupied framework or platform, broad enough for all, eligible to every farmer and mechanic—to the female equally with the male—a towering Selfhood, not physically perfect only—not satisfied with the mere mind's and learning's stores, but Religious, possessing the idea of the Infinite, (rudder and compass sure amid this troublous voyage, o'er darkest, wildest wave, through stormiest wind, of man's or nation's progress,) —realizing, above the rest, that known humanity, in deepest sense, is fair adhesion to Itself, for purposes beyond—and that, finally, the Personality of mortal life is most important with reference to the immortal, the Unknown, the Spiritual, the only permanently real, which, as the ocean waits for and receives the rivers, waits for us each and all.

Much is there, yet, demanding line and outline in our Vistas, not only on these topics, but others quite unwritten. Indeed, we could talk the matter, and expand it, through lifetime. But it is necessary to return to our original premises. In view of them, we have again pointedly to confess that all the objective grandeurs of the World, for highest purposes, yield themselves up, and depend on mentality alone. Here, and here only, all balances, all rests. For the mind, which alone builds the permanent edifice, haughtily builds it to itself. By it, with what follows it, are conveyed to mortal sense the culminations of the materialistic, the known, and a prophecy of the unknown. To take expression, to incarnate, to endow a Literature with grand and archetypal models—to fill with pride and love the utmost capacity, and to achieve spiritual meanings, and suggest the future—these, and these only, satisfy the soul. We must not say one word against real materials ; but the wise know that they do not become real till touched by emotions, the mind. Did we call the latter imponderable? Ah, let us rather proclaim that the slightest song-tune, the countless ephemera of passions aroused by orators and tale-tellers, are more dense, more weighty than the engines there in the great factories, or the granite blocks in their foundations.

—Approaching thus the momentous spaces, and considering with reference to a new and greater Personalism, the needs and possibilities of American imaginative literature, through the medium-light of what we have already broached, it will at once be appreciated that a vast gulf of difference separates the present accepted condition of these spaces, inclusive of what is floating in them, from any condition adjusted to, or fit for, the world, the America, there sought to be indicated, and the copious races of complete men and women, down along these Vistas crudely outlined.

It is, in some sort, no less a difference than lies between that long-continued nebular state and vagueness of the astronomical worlds, compared with the subsequent state, the definitely-formed worlds themselves, duly compacted, clustering in systems, hung up there, chandeliers of the universe, beholding and mutually lit by each other's lights, serving for ground of all substantial foothold, all vulgar uses—yet serving still more as an undying chain and echelon of spiritual proofs and shows. A boundless field to fill! A new Creation, with needed orbic works launched forth, to revolve in free and lawful circuits—to move, self-poised, through the ether, and shine, like heaven's own suns! With such, and nothing less, we suggest that New World Litera-
3

ture, fit to rise upon, cohere, and signalize, in time, These States.

What, however, do we more definitely mean by New World Literature? Are we not doing well enough here already? Are not the United States this day busily using, working, more printer's type, more presses, than any other country? uttering and absorbing more publications than any other? Do not our publishers fatten quicker and deeper? (helping themselves, under shelter of a delusive and sneaking law, or rather absence of law, to most of their forage, poetical, pictorial, historical, romantic, even comic, without money and without price—and fiercely resisting even the timidest proposal to pay for it.)

Many will come under this delusion—but my purpose is to dispel it. I say that a nation may hold and circulate rivers and oceans of very readable print, journals, magazines, novels, library-books, "poetry," &c.—such as The States to-day possess and circulate—of unquestionable aid and value—hundreds of new volumes annually composed and brought out here, respectable enough, indeed unsurpassed in smartness and erudition—with further hundreds, or rather millions, (as by free forage, or theft, aforementioned,) also thrown into the market,—And yet, all the while, the said nation, land, strictly speaking, may possess no literature at all.

Repeating our inquiry, What, then, do we mean by real literature? especially, the American literature of the future? Hard questions to meet. The clues are inferential, and turn us to the past. At best, we can only offer suggestions, comparisons, circuits.

—It must still be reiterated, as, for the purpose of these Memoranda, the deep lesson of History and Time, that all else in the contributions of a nation or age, through its politics, materials, heroic personalities, military eclat, &c., remains crude, and defers, in any close and thorough-going estimate, until vitalized by national, original archetypes in literature. They only put the nation in form, finally tell anything, prove, complete anything—perpetuate anything. Without doubt, some of the richest and most powerful and populous communities of the antique world, and some of the grandest personalities and events, have, to after and present times, left themselves entirely unbequeathed. Doubtless, greater than any that have come down to us, were among those lands, heroisms, persons, that have not come down to us at all, even by name, date, or location. Others have arrived safely, as from voyages over wide, centuries-stretching seas. The little ships, the miracles that have buoyed them, and by incredible chances safely conveyed them, (or the best of them, their meaning and essence,) over long wastes, darkness, lethargy, ignorance, &c., have been a few inscriptions—a few immortal compositions, small in size, yet compassing what measureless values of reminiscence, contemporary portraitures, manners, idioms and beliefs, with deepest inference, hint and thought, to tie and touch forever the old, new body, and the old, new soul. These! and still these! bearing the freight so dear—dearer than pride— dearer than love. All the best experience of humanity, folded, saved, freighted to us here! Some of these tiny ships we call Old and New Testament, Homer, Eschylus, Plato, Juvenal, &c. Precious minims! I think, if we were forced to choose, rather than have you, and the likes of you, and what belongs to, and has grown of you, blotted out and gone, we could better afford, appalling as that would be, to lose all actual ships, this day fastened by wharf, or floating on wave, and see them, with all their cargoes, scuttled and sent to the bottom.

Gathered by geniuses of city, race, or age, and put by them in highest of art's forms, namely, the literary form, the peculiar combinations, and the outshows of that city, age, or race, its particular modes of the universal attributes and passions, its faiths, heroes, lovers and gods, wars, traditions, struggles, crimes, emotions, joys, (or the subtle spirit of these,) having been passed on to us to illumine our own selfhood, and its experiences—what they supply, indispensable and highest, if taken away, nothing else in all the world's boundless store-houses could make up to us, or ever again return.

For us, along the great highways of time, those monuments stand—those forms of majesty and beauty. For us those beacons burn through all the nights. Unknown Egyptians, graving hieroglyphs; Hindus, with hymn and apothegm and endless epic; Hebrew prophet, with spirituality, as in flashes of lightning, conscience, like red-hot iron, plaintive songs and screams of vengeance for tyrannies and enslavement; Christ, with bent head, brooding love and peace, like a dove; Greek, creating eternal shapes of physical and esthetic proportion; Roman, lord of satire, the sword, and the codex;—of the figures, some far-off and veiled, others nearer and visible; Dante, stalking with lean form, nothing but fibre, not a grain of superfluous flesh; Angelo, and the great painters, architects, musicians; rich Shakespeare, luxuriant as the sun, artist and singer of Feudalism in its sunset, with all the gorgeous colors, owner thereof, and using them at will;—and so to such as German Kant and Hegel, where they, though near us, leaping over the ages, sit again, impassive, imperturbable, like the Egyptian gods. Of these, and the like of these, is it too much, indeed, to return to our favorite figure, and view them as orbs and systems of orbs, moving in free paths in the spaces of that other heaven, the kosmic intellect, the Soul?

Ye powerful and resplendent ones! ye were, in your atmospheres, grown not for America, but rather for her foes, the Feudal and the old—while our genius is Democratic and modern. Yet could ye, indeed, but breathe your breath of life into our New World's nostrils—not to enslave us, as now, but, for our needs, to breed a spirit like your own—perhaps, (dare we to say it?) to dominate, even destroy, what you yourselves have left! On your plane, and no less, but even higher and wider, will I mete and measure for our wants to-day and here. I demand races of orbic bards, with unconditional, uncompromising sway. Come forth, sweet democratic despots of the west!

By points and specimens like these we, in reflection, token what we mean by any land's or people's genuine literature. And thus compared and tested, judging amid the influence of loftiest products only, what do our current copious fields of print, covering, in manifold forms, the United States, better, for an analogy, present, than, as in certain regions of the sea, those spreading, undulating masses of squid, through which the whale, swimming with head half out, feeds?

Not but that doubtless our current so-called literature, (like an endless supply of small coin,) performs a certain service, and may-be, too, the service needed for the time, (the preparation service, as children learn to spell.) Everybody reads, and truly nearly everybody writes, either books, or for the magazines or journals. The matter has magnitude, too, after a sort. There is something impressive about the huge editions of the dailies and weeklies, the mountain-stacks of white paper piled in the press-vaults, and the proud, crashing, ten-cylinder presses, which I can stand and watch any time by the half hour. Then, (though The States in the field of Imagination present not a single first-class work, not a single great Literatus,) the main objects, to amuse, to titillate, to pass away time, to circulate the news and rumors of news, to rhyme and read rhyme, are yet attained, and on a scale of infinity. To-day, in books, in the rivalry of writers, especially novelists, success, (so-called,) is for him or her who strikes the mean flat average, the sensational appetite for stimulus, incident, &c., and depicts, to the common calibre, sensual, exterior life. To such, or the luckiest of them, as we see, the audiences are limitless and profitable; but they cease presently. While, this day or any day, to workmen, portraying interior or spiritual life, the audiences were limited, and often laggard—but they last forever.

—Compared with the past, our modern science soars, and our journals serve; but ideal and even ordinary romantic literature does not, I think, substantially advance. Behold the prolific brood of the contemporary novel, magazine-tale, theatre-play, &c. The same endless thread of tangled and superlative love-story, inherited, apparently, from the Amadises and Palmerins of the 13th, 14th and 15th centuries over there in Europe. The costumes and associations are brought down to date, the seasoning is hotter and more varied, the dragons and ogres are left out—but the *thing*, I should say, has not advanced—is just as sensational, just as strained—remains about the 'same, nor more, nor less.

—What is the reason, our time, our lands, that we see no fresh local courage, sanity, of our own—the Mississippi, stalwart Western men, real mental and physical facts, Southerners, &c., in the body of our literature? especially the poetic part of it. But always, instead, a parcel of dandies and ennuyees, dapper little gentlemen from abroad, who flood us with their thin sentiment of parlors, parasols, piano-songs, tinkling rhymes, the five-hundredth importation, or whimpering and crying about something, chasing one aborted conceit after another, and forever occupied in dyspeptic amours with dyspeptic women.

While, current and novel, the grandest events and revolutions, and stormiest passions of history, are crossing to-day with unparalleled rapidity and magnificence over the stages of our own and all the continents, offering new materials, opening new vistas, with largest needs, inviting the daring launching forth of conceptions in Literature, inspired by them, soaring in highest regions, serving Art in its highest, (which is only the other name for serving God, and serving Humanity,) where is the man of letters, where is the book, with any nobler aim than to follow in the old track, repeat what has been said before—and, as its utmost triumph, sell well, and be erudite or elegant?

Mark the roads, the processes, through which These States have arrived, standing easy, ever-equal, ever-compact, in their range, to-day. European adventures? the most antique? Asiatic or African? old history—miracles—romances? Rather, our own unquestioned facts. They hasten, incredible, blazing bright as fire. From the deeds and days of Columbus down to the present, and including the present—and especially the late Secession war—when I con them, I feel, every leaf, like stopping to see if I have not made a mistake, and fallen upon the splendid figments of some dream.

But it is no dream. We stand, live, move, in the huge flow of our age's materialism—in its spirituality. We have had founded for us the most positive of lands. The founders have passed to other spheres—But what are these terrible duties they have left us?

Their politics the United States have, in my opinion, with all their faults, already substantially established, for good, on their own native, sound, long-vista'd principles, never to be overturned, offering a sure basis for all the rest. With that, their future religious forms, sociology, literature, teachers, schools, costumes, &c., are of course to make a compact whole, uniform, on tallying principles. For how can we remain, divided, contradicting ourselves, this way? * I say we can only attain harmony and stability by consulting ensemble, and the ethic purports, and faithfully building upon them.

For the New World, indeed, after two grand stages of preparation-strata, I perceive that now, a third stage, being ready for, (and without which the other two were useless,) with unmistakable signs appears. The First Stage was the planning and putting on record the political foundation rights of immense masses of people— indeed all people—in the organization of Republican National, State, and Municipal governments, all constructed with reference to each, and each to all. This is the American programme, not for classes, but for universal man, and is embodied in the compacts of the

---

* Note, to-day, an instructive, curious spectacle and conflict. Science, (twin, in its fields, of Democracy in its)—Science, testing absolutely all thoughts, all works, has already burst well upon the world—a Sun, mounting, most illuminating, most glorious— surely never again to set. But against it, deeply entrenched, holding possession, yet remains, (not only through the churches and schools, but by imaginative literature, and unregenerate poetry,) the fossil theology of the mythic-materialistic, superstitious, untaught and credulous, fable-loving, primitive ages of humanity.

Declaration of Independence, and, as it began and has
now grown, with its amendments, the Federal Constitution—and in the State governments, with all their
interiors, and with general suffrage ; those having the
sense not only of what is in themselves, but that their
certain several things started, planted, hundreds of
others, in the same direction, duly arise and follow.
The Second Stage relates to material prosperity, wealth,
produce, labor-saving machines, iron, cotton, local, State
and continental railways, intercommunication and trade
with all lands, steamships, mining, general employment,
organization of great cities, cheap appliances for comfort, numberless technical schools, books, newspapers,
a currency for money circulation, &c. The Third Stage,
rising out of the previous ones, to make them and all
illustrious, I, now, for one, promulge, announcing a native Expression Spirit, getting into form, adult, and
through mentality, for These States, self-contained, different from others, more expansive, more rich and free,
to be evidenced by original authors and poets to come,
by American personalities, plenty of them, male and
female, traversing the States, none excepted—and by
native superber tableaux and growths of language,
songs, operas, orations, lectures, architecture—and by
a sublime and serious Religious Democracy sternly
taking command, dissolving the old, sloughing off surfaces, and from its own interior and vital principles,
entirely reconstructing Society.

—For America, type of progress, and of essential
faith in Man—above all his errors and wickedness—
few suspect how deep, how deep it really strikes. The
world evidently supposes, and we have evidently supposed so too, that The States are merely to achieve the
equal franchise, an elective government—to inaugurate
the respectability of labor, and become a nation of practical operatives, law-abiding, orderly and well-off. Yes,
those are indeed parts of the tasks of America ; but
they not only do not exhaust the progressive conception, but rather arise, teeming with it, as the mediums
of deeper, higher progress. Daughter of a physical
revolution—Mother of the true revolutions, which are

of the interior life, and of the arts. For so long as the spirit is not changed, any change of appearance is of no avail.

—The old men, I remember as a boy, were always talking of American Independence. What is independence? Freedom from all laws or bonds except those of one's own being, controlled by the universal ones. To lands, to man, to woman, what is there at last to each, but the inherent soul, nativity, idiocrasy, free, highest-poised, soaring its own flight, following out itself?

—At present, These States, in their theology and social standards, &c., (of greater importance than their political institutions,) are entirely held possession of by foreign lands. We see the sons and daughters of the New World, ignorant of its genius, not yet inaugurating the native, the universal, and the near, still importing the distant, the partial, and the dead. We see London, Paris, Italy—not original, superb, as where they belong—but second-hand here where they do not belong. We see the shreds of Hebrews, Romans, Greeks; but where, on her own soil, do we see, in any faithful, highest, proud expression, America herself? I sometimes question whether she has a corner in her own house.

Not but that in one sense, and a very grand one, good theology, good Art, or good Literature, has certain features shared in common. The combination fraternizes, ties the races—is, in many particulars, under laws applicable indifferently to all, irrespective of climate or date, and, from whatever source, appeals to emotions, pride, love, spirituality, common to humankind. Nevertheless, they touch a man closest, (perhaps only actually touch him,) even in these, in their expression through autochthonic lights and shades, flavors, fondnesses, aversions, specific incidents, illustrations, out of his own nationality, geography, surroundings, antecedents, &c. The spirit and the form are one, and depend far more on association, identity and place, than is supposed. Subtly interwoven with the materiality and personality of a land, a race—Teuton, Turk, Californian, or what not—there is always something—I can hardly tell what

it is,—History but describes the results of it,—it is the
same as the untellable look of some human faces.   Nature, too, in her stolid forms, is full of it—but to most
it is there a secret.   This something is rooted in the invisible roots, the profoundest meanings of that place,
race, or nationality ; and to absorb and again effuse it,
uttering words and products as from its midst, and carrying it into highest regions, is the work, or a main part
of the work, of any country's true author, poet, historian, lecturer, and perhaps even priest and philosoph.
Here, and here only, are the foundations for our really
valuable and permanent verse, drama, &c.

But at present, (judged by any higher scale than that
which finds the chief ends of existence to be to fever-
ishly make money during one-half of it, and by some
" amusement," or perhaps foreign travel, flippantly kill
time, the other half,) and considered with reference to
purposes of patriotism, health, a noble Personality, religion, and the democratic adjustments, all these swarms
of poems, dramatic plays, resultant so far from American intellect, and the formulation of our best ideas, are
useless and a mockery.   They strengthen and nourish
no one, express nothing characteristic, give decision and
purpose to no one, and suffice only the lowest level of
vacant minds.

Of the question, indeed, of what is called the Drama,
or dramatic presentation in the United States, as now
put forth at the theatres, I should say it deserves to be
treated with the same gravity, and on a par with the
questions of ornamental confectionery at public dinners,
or the arrangement of curtains and hangings in a ball-
room—nor more, nor less.

Of the other, I will not insult the reader's intelligence, (once really entering into the atmosphere of
these Vistas,) by supposing it necessary to show, in detail, why the copious dribble, either of our little or well-
known rhymesters, does not fulfil, in any respect, the
needs and august occasions of this land.   America demands a Poetry that is bold, modern, and all-surround-
ing and kosmical, as she is herself.   It must in no respect ignore science or the modern, but inspire itself

with science and the modern. It must bend its vision toward the future, more than the past. Like America, it must extricate itself from even the greatest models of the past, and, while courteous to them, must have entire faith in itself and products out of its own original spirit only. Like her, it must place in the van, and hold up at all hazards, the banner of the divine pride of man in himself, (the radical foundation of the new religion.) Long enough have the People been listening to poems in which common Humanity, deferential, bends low, humiliated, acknowledging superiors. But America listens to no such poems. Erect, inflated, and fully self-esteeming be the chant; and then America will listen with pleased ears.

—Nor may the genuine gold, the gems, when brought to light at last, be probably ushered forth from any of the quarters currently counted on. To-day, doubtless, the infant Genius of American poetic expression, (eluding those highly-refined imported and gilt-edged themes, and sentimental and butterfly flights, pleasant to New York, Boston, and Philadelphia publishers—causing tender spasms in the coteries, and warranted not to chafe the sensitive cuticle of the most exquisitely artificial gossamer delicacy,) lies sleeping far away, happily unrecognized and uninjured by the coteries, the art-writers, the talkers and critics of the saloons, or the lecturers in the colleges—lies sleeping, aside, unrecking itself, in some Western idiom, or native Michigan or Tennessee repartee, or stump-speech—or in Kentucky or Georgia or the Carolinas—or in some slang or local song or allusion of the Manhattan, Boston, Philadelphia or Baltimore mechanic—or up in the Maine woods—or off in the hut of the California miner, or crossing the Rocky mountains, or along the Pacific railroad—or on the breasts of the young farmers of the Northwest, or Canada, or boatmen of the lakes. Rude and coarse nursing-beds these; but only from such beginnings and stocks, indigenous here, may haply arrive, be grafted, and sprout, in time, flowers of genuine American aroma, and fruits truly and fully our own.

—I say it were a standing disgrace to These States—

I say it were a disgrace to any nation, distinguished
above others by the variety and vastness of its territories, its materials, its inventive activity, and the splendid
practicality of its people, not to rise and soar above
others also in its original styles in literature and art,
and its own supply of intellectual and esthetic master-
pieces, archetypal, and consistent with itself. I know
not a land except ours that has not, to some extent,
however small, made its title clear. The Scotch have
their born ballads, tunes subtly expressing their past
and present, and expressing character. The Irish have
theirs. England, Italy, France, Spain, theirs. What
has America? With exhaustless mines of the richest
ore of epic, lyric, tale, tune, picture, &c., in the Four
Years' War; with, indeed, I sometimes think, the richest
masses of material ever afforded a nation, more variegated, and on a larger scale—the first sign of proportionate, native, imaginative Soul, and first-class works
to match, is, (I cannot too often repeat,) so far wanting.

Long ere the Second Centennial arrives, there
will be some Forty to Fifty great States, among them
Canada and Cuba. The population will be sixty or seventy millions. The Pacific will be ours, and the Atlantic
mainly ours. There will be daily electric communication with every part of the globe. What an age! What
a land! Where, elsewhere, one so great? The Individuality of one nation must then, as always, lead the
world. Can there be any doubt who the leader ought
to be? Bear in mind, though, that nothing less than
the mightiest original non-subordinated SOUL has ever
really, gloriously led, or ever can lead. (This Soul—
its other name, in these Vistas, is LITERATURE.)

In fond fancy leaping those hundred years ahead, let
us survey America's works, poems, philosophies, fulfilling prophecies, and giving form and decision to best
ideals. Much that is now undreamed of, we might then
perhaps see established, luxuriantly cropping forth, rich-
ness, vigor of letters and of artistic expression, in whose
products character will be a main requirement, and not
merely erudition or elegance.

Intense and loving comradeship, the personal and passionate attachment of man to man—which, hard to define, underlies the lessons and ideals of the profound saviours of every land and age, and which seems to promise, when thoroughly developed, cultivated and recognized in manners and Literature, the most substantial hope and safety of the future of These States, will then be fully expressed.*

A strong-fibred Joyousness, and Faith, and the sense of Health *al fresco,* may well enter into the preparation of future noble American authorship. Part of the test of a great Literatus shall be the absence in him of the idea of the covert, the artificial, the lurid, the maleficent, the devil, the grim estimates inherited from the Puritans, hell, natural depravity, and the like. The great Literatus will be known, among the rest, by his cheerful simplicity, his adherence to natural standards, his limitless faith in God, his reverence, and by the absence in him of doubt, ennui, burlesque, persiflage, or any strained and temporary fashion.

Nor must I fail, again and yet again, to clinch, reiterate more plainly still, (O that indeed such survey as we fancy, may show in time this part completed also!) the lofty aim, surely the proudest and the purest, in whose service the future Literatus, of whatever field, may gladly labor. As we have intimated, offsetting the

---

* It is to the development, identification, and general prevalence of that fervid comradeship, (the adhesive love, at least rivaling the amative love hitherto possessing imaginative literature, if not going beyond it,) that I look for the counterbalance and offset of our materialistic and vulgar American Democracy, and for the spiritualization thereof. Many will say it is a dream, and will not follow my inferences; but I confidently expect a time when there will be seen, running like a half-hid warp through all the myriad audible and visible worldly interests of America, threads of manly friendship, fond and loving, pure and sweet, strong and life-long, carried to degrees hitherto unknown—not only giving tone to individual character, and making it unprecedently emotional, muscular, heroic, and refined, but having deepest relations to general politics. I say Democracy infers such loving comradeship, as its most inevitable twin or counterpart, without which it will be incomplete, in vain, and incapable of perpetuating itself.

material civilization of our race, our Nationality, its
wealth, territories, factories, population, luxuries, products, trade, and military and naval strength, and
breathing breath of life into all these, and more, must
be its Moral Civilization—the formulation, expression,
and aidancy whereof, is the very highest height of literature. And still within this wheel, revolves another
wheel. The climax of this loftiest range of modern
civilization, giving finish and hue, and rising above all
tho gorgoous shows and results of wealth, intellect,
power, and art, as such—above even theology and religious fervor—is to be its development, from the eternal
bases, and the fit expression, of absolute Conscience,
moral soundness, Justice. I say there is nothing else
higher, for Nation, Individual, or for Literature, than
the idea, and practical realization and expression of the
idea, of Conscience, kept at topmost mark, absolute in
itself, well cultivated, uncontaminated by the manifold
weeds, the cheats, changes, and vulgarities of the fash-
ions of the world. Even in religious fervor there is a
touch of animal heat. But moral conscientiousness,
crystalline, without flaw, not Godlike only, entirely
Human, awes and enchants me forever. Great is emotional Love, even in the order of the rational universe.
But, if we must make gradations, I am clear there is
something greater. Power, love, veneration, products,
genius, esthetics, tried by subtlest comparisons, analyses,
and in serenest moods, somewhere fail, somehow become vain. Then noiseless, with flowing steps, the lord,
the sun, the last Ideal comes. By the names Right,
Justice, Truth, we suggest, but do not describe it. To
the world of men it remains a dream, an idea as they
call it. But no dream is it to the wise—but the proudest, almost only solid lasting thing of all.

I say, again and forever, the triumph of America's
democratic formules is to be the inauguration, growth,
acceptance, and unmistakable supremacy among individuals, cities, States, and the Nation, of moral Conscience. Its analogy in the material universe is what
holds together this world, and every object upon it, and
carries its dynamics on forever sure and safe. Its lack,

and the persistent shirking of it, as in life, sociology, literature, politics, business, and even sermonizing, these times, or any times, still leaves the abysm, the mortal flaw and smutch, mocking civilization to-day, with all its unquestioned triumphs, and all the civilization so far known. Such is the thought I would especially bequeath to any earnest persons, students of these Vistas, and following after me.*

Present Literature, while magnificently fulfilling certain popular demands, with plenteous knowledge and verbal smartness, is profoundly sophisticated, insane, and its very joy is morbid. It needs retain the knowledge, and fulfil the demands, but needs to purge itself; or rather needs to be born again, become unsophisticated, and become sane. It needs tally and express Nature, and the spirit of Nature, and to know and obey the standards. I say the question of Nature, largely considered, involves the questions of the esthetic, the emotional, and the religious—and involves happiness. A fitly born and bred race, growing up in right condi-

---

* I am reminded as I write that out of this very Conscience, or idea of Conscience, of intense moral right, and in its name and strained construction, the worst fanaticisms, wars, persecutions, murders, &c., have yet, in all lands, been broached, and have come to their devilish fruition. Much is to be said—but I may say here, and in response, that side by side with the unflagging stimulation of the elements of Religion and Conscience must henceforth move with equal sway, science, absolute reason, and the general proportionate development of the whole man. These scientific facts, deductions, are divine too—precious counted parts of moral civilization, and, with physical health, indispensable to it, to prevent fanaticism. For Abstract Religion, I perceive, is easily led astray, ever credulous, and is capable of devouring, remorseless, like fire and flame. Conscience, too, isolated from all else, and from the emotional nature, may but attain the beauty and purity of glacial, snowy ice. We want, for These States, for the general character, a cheerful, religious fervor, enhued with the ever-present modifications of the human emotions, friendship, benevolence, with a fair field for scientific inquiry, the right of individual judgment, and always the cooling influences of material Nature. We want not again either the religious fervor of the Spanish Inquisition, nor the morality of the New England Puritans.

tions of out-door as much as in-door harmony, activity, and development, would probably, from and in
those conditions, find it enough merely *to live*—and
would, in their relations to the sky, air, water, trees,
&c., and to the countless common shows, and in the
fact of Life itself, discover and achieve happiness—
with Being suffused night and day by wholesome
extasy, surpassing all the pleasures that wealth, amusement, and even gratified intellect, erudition, or the sense
of art, can give.

In the prophetic literature of These States, Nature,
true Nature, and the true idea of Nature, long absent,
must, above all, become fully restored, enlarged, and
must furnish the pervading atmosphere to poems, and
the test of all high literary and esthetic compositions.
I do not mean the smooth walks, trimm'd hedges, but-
terflies, poseys and nightingales of the English poets,
but the whole Orb, with its geologic history, the Kosmos,
carrying fire and snow, that rolls through the illimitable
areas, light as a feather, though weighing billions of
tons. Furthermore, as by what we now partially call
Nature is intended, at most, only what is entertainable
by the physical conscience, the lessons of the esthetic,
the sense of matter, and of good animal health—on
these it must be distinctly accumulated, incorporated,
that man, comprehending these, has, in towering super-
addition, the Moral and Spiritual Consciences, indicating his destination beyond the ostensible, the mortal.

To the heights of such estimate of Nature indeed
ascending, we proceed to make observations for our
Vistas, breathing rarest air. What is I believe called
Idealism seems to me to suggest, (guarding against extravagance, and ever modified even by its opposite,) the
course of inquiry and desert of favor for our New World
metaphysics, their foundation of and in literature, giving hue to all.*

---

* The culmination and fruit of literary artistic expression, and
its final fields of pleasure for the human soul, are in Metaphysics,
including the mysteries of the spiritual world, the soul itself, and
the question of the immortal continuation of our identity. In all
ages, the mind of man has brought up here—and always will.

The elevating and etherealizing ideas of the Unknown and of Unreality must be brought forward with au-

Here, at least, of whatever race or era, we stand on common ground. Applause, too, is unanimous, antique or modern. Those authors who work well in this field—though their reward, instead of a handsome percentage, or royalty, may be but simply the laurel-crown of the victors in the great Olympic games—will be dearest to humanity, and their works, however esthetically defective, will be treasured forever. The altitude of literature and poetry has always been Religion—and always will be. The Indian Vedas, the Naçkas of Zoroaster, The Talmud of the Jews, the Old Testament also, the Gospel of Christ and his disciples, Plato's works, the Koran of Mohammed, the Edda of Snorro, and so on toward our own day, to Swedenborg, and to the invaluable contributions of Leibnitz, Kant and Hegel,—these, with such poems only in which, (while singing well of persons and events, of the passions of man, and the shows of the material universe,) the religious tone, the consciousness of mystery, the recognition of the future, of the unknown, of Deity, over and under all, and of the divine purpose, are never absent, but indirectly give tone to all—exhibit literature's real heights and elevations, towering up like the great mountains of the earth.

Standing on this ground—the last, the highest, only permanent ground—and sternly criticising, from it, all works, either of the literary, or any Art, we have peremptorily to dismiss every pretensive production, however fine its esthetic or intellectual points, which violates, or ignores, or even does not celebrate, the central Divine Idea of All, suffusing universe, of eternal trains of purpose, in the development, by however slow degrees, of the physical, moral, and spiritual Kosmos. I say he has studied, meditated to no profit, whatever may be his mere erudition, who has not absorbed this simple consciousness and faith. It is not entirely new—but it is for America to elaborate it, and look to build upon and expand from it, with uncompromising reliance. Above the doors of teaching the inscription is to appear, Though little or nothing can be absolutely known, perceived, except from a point of view which is evanescent, yet we know at least one permanency, that Time and Space, in the will of God, furnish successive chains, completions of material births and beginnings, solve all discrepancies, fears and doubts, and eventually fulfil happiness— and that the prophecy of those births, namely Spiritual results, throws the true arch over all teaching, all science. The local considerations of sin, disease, deformity, ignorance, death, &c., and their measurement by superficial mind, and ordinary legislation and theology, are to be met by Science, boldly accepting, promulging this faith, and planting the seeds of superber laws— of the explication of the physical universe through the spiritual— and clearing the way for a Religion, sweet and unimpugnable alike to little child or great savan.

thority, as they are the legitimate heirs of the known,
and of reality, and at least as great as their parents.
Fearless of scoffing, and of the ostent, let us take our
stand, our ground, and never desert it, to confront the
growing excess and arrogance of Realism.   To the cry,
now victorious—the cry of Sense, science, flesh, in-
comes, farms, merchandise, logic, intellect, demonstra-
tions, solid perpetuities, buildings of brick and iron, or
even the facts of the shows of trees, earth, rocks, &c.,
fear not my brethren, my sisters, to sound out with
equally determined voice, that conviction brooding
within the recesses of every envisioned soul—Illusions!
apparitions! figments all!   True, we must not condemn
the show, neither absolutely deny it, for the indispensa-
bility of its meanings ; but how clearly we see that,
migrate in soul to what we can already conceive of superior and spiritual points of view, and, palpable as it
seems under present relations, it all and several might,
nay certainly would, fall apart and vanish.

—I hail with joy the oceanic, variegated, intense
practical energy, the demand for facts, even the business materialism of the current age, Our States.   But
wo to the age or land in which these things, movements,
stopping at themselves, do not tend to ideas.   As fuel
to flame, and flame to the heavens, so must wealth,
science, materialism, unerringly feed the highest mind,
the soul.   Infinitude the flight : fathomless the mystery.
Man, so diminutive, dilates beyond the sensible universe, competes with, outcopes Space and Time, medi-
tating even one great idea.   Thus, and thus only, does
a human being, his spirit, ascend above, and justify,
objective Nature, which, probably nothing in itself, is
incredibly and divinely serviceable, indispensable, real,
here.   And as the purport of objective Nature is doubtless folded, hidden, somewhere here—As somewhere
here is what this globe and its manifold forms, and the
light of day, and night's darkness, and life itself, with
all its experiences, are for—it is here the great Literature, especially verse, must get its inspiration and throbbing blood.   Then may we attain to a poetry worthy

the immortal soul of man, and which while absorbing
materials, and, in their own sense, the shows of Nature,
will, above all, have, both directly and indirectly, a freeing, fluidizing, expanding, religious character, exulting
with science, fructifying the moral elements, and stimu-
lating aspirations, and meditations on the unknown.

The process, so far, is indirect and peculiar, and
though it may be suggested, cannot be defined. Observing, rapport, and with intuition, the shows and
forms presented by Nature, the sensuous luxuriance,
the beautiful in living men and women, the actual play
of passions, in history and life—and, above all, from
those developments either in Nature or human personality in which power, (dearest of all to the sense of tha
artist,) transacts itself—Out of these, and seizing what
is in them, the poet, the esthetic worker in any field,
by the divine magic of his genius, projects them, their
analogies, by curious removes, indirections, in Literature and Art. (No useless attempt to repeat the material creation, by daguerreotyping the exact likeness by
mortal mental means.) This is the image-making faculty, coping with material creation, and rivaling, almost
triumphing over it. This alone, when all the other parts
of a specimen of literature or art are ready and waiting,
can breathe into it the breath of life, and endow it with
Identity.

"The true question to ask," says the Librarian of
Congress in a paper read before the Social Science
Convention at New York, October, 1869, "The true
question to ask respecting a book, is, *Has it helped any
human Soul?*" This is the hint, statement, not only of
the great Literatus, his book, but of every great Artist.

It may be that all works of art are to be first tried by
their art qualities, their image-forming talent, and their
dramatic, pictorial, plot-constructing, euphonious and
other talents. Then, whenever claiming to be first-class
works, they are to be strictly and sternly tried by their
foundation in, and radiation, in the highest sense, and
always indirectly, of the ethic principles, and eligibility
to free, arouse, dilate.

As within the purposes of the Kosmos, and vivifying

all meteorology, and all the congeries of the mineral, vegetable and animal worlds—all the physical growth and development of man, and all the history of the race in politics, religions, wars, &c., there is a moral purpose, a visible or invisible intention, certainly underlying all— its results and proof needing to be patiently waited for— needing intuition, faith, idiosyncrasy, to its realization, which many, and especially the intellectual, do not have —so in the product, or congeries of the product, of the greatest Literatus. This is the last, profoundest meas ure and test of a first-class literary or esthetic achieve- ment, and when understood and put in force must fain, I say, lead to works, books, nobler than any hitherto known. Lo! Nature, (the only complete, actual poem,) existing calmly in the divine scheme, containing all, content, careless of the criticisms of a day, or these endless and wordy chatterers. And lo! to the con- sciousness of the soul, the permanent Identity, the thought, the something, before which the magnitude even of Democracy, Art, Literature, &c., dwindles, be- comes partial, measurable—something that fully satis- fies, (which those do not.) That something is the All, and the idea of All, with the accompanying idea of Eternity, and of itself, the Soul, buoyant, indestructi- ble, sailing space forever, visiting every region, as a ship the sea. And again lo! the pulsations in all matter, all spirit, throbbing forever—the eternal beats, eternal systole and diastole of life in things—where- from I feel and know that death is not the ending, as was thought, but rather the real beginning—and that nothing ever is or can be lost, nor ever die, nor soul, nor matter.

—I say in the future of These States must therefore arise Poets immenser far, and make great poems of Death. The poems of Life are great, but there must be the poems of the purports of life, not only in itself, but beyond itself. I have eulogized Homer, the sacred bards of Jewry, Eschylus, Juvenal, Shakespeare, &c., and acknowledged their inestimable value. But, (with perhaps the exception, in some, not all respects, of the second mentioned,) I say there must, for future and

Democratic purposes, appear poets, (dare I to say so?) of higher class even than any of those—poets not only possessed of the religious fire and abandon of Isaiah, luxuriant in the epic talent of Homer, or for characters as Shakespeare, but consistent with the Hegelian formulas, and consistent with modern science. America needs, and the world needs, a class of bards who will, now and ever, so link and tally the rational physical being of man, with the ensembles of Time and Space, and with this vast and multiform show, Nature, surrounding him, ever tantalizing him, equally a part, and yet not a part of him, as to essentially harmonize, satisfy, and put at rest. Faith, very old, now scared away by science, must be restored, brought back, by the same power that caused her departure—restored with new sway, deeper, wider, higher than ever. Surely, this universal ennui, this coward fear, this shuddering at death, these low, degrading views, are not always to rule the spirit pervading future society, as it has the past, and does the present. What the Roman Lucretius sought most nobly, yet all too blindly, negatively to do for his age and its successors, must be done positively by some great coming Literatus, especially Poet, who, while remaining fully poet, will absorb whatever science indicates, with spiritualism, and out of them, and out of his own genius, will compose the great Poem of Death. Then will man indeed confront Nature, and confront Time and Space, both with science and *con amore*, and take his right place, prepared for life, master of fortune and misfortune. And then that which was long wanted will be supplied, and the ship that had it not before in all her voyages, will have an anchor.

There are still other standards, suggestions, for products of high literatuses. That which really balances and conserves the social and political world is not so much legislation, police, treaties, and dread of punishment, as the latent eternal intuitional sense, in humanity, of fairness, manliness, decorum, &c. Indeed, the perennial regulation, control and oversight, by self-suppliance, is *sine qua non* to Democracy; and a highest,

widest aim of Democratic literature may well be to
bring forth, cultivate, brace and strengthen this sense
in individuals and society.   A strong mastership of the
general inferior self by the superior self, is to be aided,
secured, indirectly but surely, by the literatus, in his
works, shaping, for individual or aggregate Democracy,
a great passionate Body, in and along with which goes
a great masterful Spirit.

   And still, providing for contingencies, I fain confront
the fact, the need of powerful native philosophs and
orators and bards, These States, as rallying points to
come, in times of danger, and to fend off ruin and de-
fection.   For history is long, long, long.   Shift and turn
the combinations of the statement as we may, the problem of the future of America is in certain respects as
dark as it is vast.   Pride, competition, segregation,
vicious wilfulness, and license beyond example, brood
already upon us.   Unwieldy and immense, who shall
hold in behemoth? who bridle leviathan?   Flaunt it as
we choose, athwart and over the roads of our progress
loom huge uncertainty, and dreadful, threatening gloom.
It is useless to deny it : Democracy grows rankly up the
thickest, noxious, deadliest plants and fruits of all—
brings worse and worse invaders—needs newer, larger,
stronger, keener compensations and compellers.
   Our lands, embracing so much, (embracing indeed
the whole, rejecting none,) hold in their breast that
flame also, capable of consuming themselves, consuming
us all.   Short as the span of our national life has been,
already have death and downfall crowded close upon
us—and will again crowd close, no doubt, even if
warded off.   Ages to come may never know, but I
know, how narrowly, during the late Secession war—
and more than once, and more than twice or thrice—
our Nationality, (wherein bound up, as in a ship in a
storm, depended, and yet depend, all our best life, all
hope, all value,) just grazed, just by a hair escaped destruction.   Alas! to think of them! the agony and
bloody sweat of certain of those hours! those cruel,
sharp, suspended crises!

Even to-day, amid these whirls, incredible flippancy, the blind fury of parties, infidelity, entire lack of first-class captains and leaders, added to the plentiful meanness and vulgarity of the ostensible masses—that problem, the Labor Question, beginning to open like a yawning gulf, rapidly widening every year *—what prospect have we? We sail a dangerous sea of seething currents, cross and under-currents, vortices—all so dark, untried—and whither shall we turn?

It seems as if the Almighty had spread before this Nation charts of imperial destinies, dazzling as the sun, yet with lines of blood, and many a deep intestine difficulty, and human aggregate of cankerous imperfection, —saying, Lo! the roads, the only plans of development,

---

* The Labor Question.—The immense problem of the relation, adjustment, conflict, between Labor and its status and pay, on the one side, and the Capital of employers on the other side—looming up over These States like an ominous, limitless, murky cloud, perhaps before long to overshadow us all;—the many thousands of decent working-people, through the cities and elsewhere, trying to keep up a good appearance, but living by daily toil, from hand to mouth, with nothing ahead. and no owned homes—the increasing aggregation of capital in the hands of a few—the chaotic confusion of labor in the Southern States, consequent on the abrogation of slavery—the Asiatic immigration on our Pacific side—the advent of new machinery, dispensing more and more with hand-work—the growing, alarming spectacle of countless squads of vagabond children, roaming everywhere the streets and wharves of the great cities, getting trained for thievery and prostitution—the hideousness and squalor of certain quarters of the cities—the advent of late years, and increasing frequency, of these pompous, nauseous, outside shows of vulgar wealth—(What a chance for a new Juvenal!)—wealth acquired perhaps by some quack, some measureless financial rogue, triply brazen in impudence, only shielding himself by his money from a shaved head, a striped dress, and a felon's cell;—and then, below all, the plausible, sugar-coated, but abnormal and sooner or later inevitably ruinous delusion and loss, of our system of inflated paper-money currency, (cause of all conceivable swindles, false standards of value, and principal breeder and bottom of those enormous fortunes for the few, and of poverty for the million)—with that other plausible and sugar-coated delusion, the theory and practice of a protective tariff, still clung to by many;—such, with plenty more, stretching themselves through many a long year, for solution, stand as huge impedimenta of America's progress.

long, and varied with all terrible balks and ebullitions.
You said in your soul, I will be empire of empires, over-
shadowing all else, past and present, putting the history of old-world dynasties, conquests, behind me, as
of no account—making a new history, the history of
Democracy, making old history a dwarf—I alone inaugurating largeness, culminating Time. If these, O
lands of America, are indeed the prizes, the determina-
tions of your Soul, be it so. But behold the cost, and
already specimens of the cost. Behold, the anguish of
suspense, existence itself wavering in the balance, uncertain whether to rise or fall ; already, close behind
you or around you, thick winrows of corpses on battle-
fields, countless maimed and sick in hospitals, treachery
among Generals, folly in the Executive and Legislative
departments, schemers, thieves everywhere—cant, credulity, make-believe everywhere. Thought you greatness was to ripen for you, like a pear? If you would
have greatness, know that you must conquer it through
ages, centuries—must pay for it with a proportionate
price. For you too, as for all lands, the struggle, the
traitor, the wily person in office, scrofulous wealth, the
surfeit of prosperity, the demonism of greed, the hell
of passion, the decay of faith, the long postponement,
the fossil-like lethargy, the ceaseless need of revolutions, prophets, thunderstorms, deaths, births, new pro-
jections and invigorations of ideas and men.

Yet I have dreamed, merged in that hidden-tangled
problem of our fate, whose long unraveling stretches
mysteriously through time—dreamed out, portrayed,
hinted already—a little or a larger Band—a band of
brave and true, unprecedented yet—armed and equipt
at every point—the members separated, it may be, by
different dates and States, or south, or north, or east,
or west—Pacific or Atlantic—a year, a century here,
and other centuries there—but always one, compact in
Soul, conscience-conserving, God-inculcating, inspired
achievers, not only in Literature, the greatest art, but
achievers in all art—a new, undying order, dynasty,
from age to age transmitted—a band, a class, at least

as fit to cope with current years, our dangers, needs, as those who, for their times, so long, so well, in armor or in cowl, upheld, and made illustrious, the Feudal, priestly world. To offset Chivalry, indeed, those vanished countless knights, and the old altars, abbeys, all their priests, ages and strings of ages, a knightlier and more sacred cause to-day demands, and shall supply, in a New World, to larger, grander work, more than the counterpart and tally of them.

Arrived now, definitely, at an apex for These Vistas, I confess that the promulgation and belief in such a class or institution—a new and greater Literatus Order —its possibility, (nay certainty,) underlies these entire speculations—and that the rest, the other parts, as superstructures, are all founded upon it. It really seems to me the condition, not only of our future national development, but of our perpetuation. In the highly artificial and materialistic bases of modern civilization, with the corresponding arrangements and methods of living, the force-infusion of intellect alone, the depraving influences of riches just as much as poverty, the absence of all high ideals in character—with the long series of tendencies, shapings, which few are strong enough to resist, and which now seem, with steam-engine speed, to be everywhere turning out the generations of humanity like uniform iron castings—all of which, as compared with the Feudal ages, we can yet do nothing better than accept, make the best of, and even welcome, upon the whole, for their oceanic practical grandeur, and their restless wholesale kneading of the masses—I say of all this tremendous and dominant play of solely materialistic bearings upon current life in the United States, with the results as already seen, accumulating, and reaching far into the future, that they must either be confronted and met by at least an equally subtle and tremendous force-infusion for purposes of Spiritualization, for the pure conscience, for genuine esthetics, and for absolute and primal Manliness and Womanliness—or else our modern civilization, with all its improvements, is in vain, and we are

4

on the road to a destiny, a status, equivalent, in this
real world, to that of the fabled damned.

—To furnish, therefore, something like escape and
foil and remedy—to restrain, with gentle but sufficient
hand, the terrors of materialistic, intellectual, and democratic civilization—to ascend to more ethereal, yet just
as real, atmospheres—to invoke and set forth ineffable
portraits of Personal Perfection, (the true, final aim of
all,) I say my eyes are fain to behold, though with
straining sight—and my spirit to prophecy far down
the vistas of These States, that Order, Class, superber,
far more efficient than any hitherto, arising. I say we
must enlarge and entirely recast the theory of noble
authorship, and conceive and put up as our model, a
Literatus—groups, series of Literatuses—not only consistent with modern science, practical, political, full of
the arts, of highest erudition—not only possessed by,
and possessors of, Democracy even—but with the equal
of the burning fire and extasy of Conscience, which have
brought down to us, over and through the centuries,
that chain of old unparalleled Judean prophets, with
their flashes of power, wisdom, and poetic beauty, lawless as lightning, indefinite—yet power, wisdom, beauty,
above all mere art, and surely, in some respects, above
all else we know of mere literature.

Prospecting thus the coming unsped days, and that
new Order in them—marking the endless train of exercise, development, unwind, in Nation as in man, which
life is for—we now proceed to note, as on the hopeful
terraces or platforms of our history, to be enacted, not
only amid peaceful growth, but amid all perturbations,
and after not a few departures, filling the vistas then,
certain most coveted, stately arrivals.

—A few years, and there will be an appropriate native grand Opera, the lusty and wide-lipp'd offspring of
Italian methods. Yet it will be no mere imitation, nor
follow precedents, any more than Nature follows precedents. Vast oval halls will be constructed, on acoustic
principles, in cities, where companies of musicians will
perform lyrical pieces, born to the people of These

States; and the people will make perfect music a part of their lives. Every phase, every trade will have its songs, beautifying those trades. Men on the land will have theirs, and men on the water theirs. Who now is ready to begin that work for America, of composing music fit for us—songs, choruses, symphonies, operas, oratorios, fully identified with the body and soul of The States? music complete in all its appointments, but in some fresh, courageous, melodious, undeniable styles— as all that is ever to permanently satisfy us must be. The composers to make such music are to learn everything that can be possibly learned in the schools and traditions of their art, and then calmly dismiss all traditions from them.

Also, a great breed of orators will one day spread over The United States, and be continued. Blessed are the people where, (the nation's Unity and Identity preserved at all hazards,) strong emergencies, throes, occur. Strong emergencies will continually occur in America, and will be provided for. Such orators are wanted as have never yet been heard upon the earth. What specimen have we had where even the physical capacities of the voice have been fully accomplished? I think there would be in the human voice, thoroughly practised and brought out, more seductive pathos than in any organ or any orchestra of stringed instruments, and a ring more impressive than that of artillery.

Also, in a few years, there will be, in the cities of These States, immense Museums, with suites of halls, containing samples and illustrations from all the places and peoples of the earth, old and new. In these halls, in the presence of these illustrations, the noblest savans will deliver lectures to thousands of young men and women, on history, natural history, the sciences, &c. History itself will get released from being that false and distant thing, that fetish it has been. It will become a friend, a venerable teacher, a live being, with hands, voice, presence. It will be disgraceful to a young person not to know chronology, geography, poems, heroes, deeds, and all the former nations, and present ones also—and it will be disgraceful in a teacher to teach any less or more than he believes.

—We see, fore-indicated, amid these prospects and hopes, new law-forces of spoken and written language —not merely the pedagogue-forms, correct, regular, familiar with precedents, made for matters of outside propriety, fine words, thoughts definitely told out—but a language fanned by the breath of Nature, which leaps overhead, cares mostly for impetus and effects, and for what it plants and invigorates to grow—tallies life and character, and seldomer tells a thing than suggests or necessitates it. In fact, a new theory of literary composition for imaginative works of the very first class, and especially for highest poems, is the sole course open to These States.

Books are to be called for, and supplied, on the assumption that the process of reading is not a half-sleep, but, in highest sense, an exercise, a gymnast's struggle ; that the reader is to do something for himself, must be on the alert, must himself or herself construct indeed the poem, argument, history, metaphysical essay—the text furnishing the hints, the clue, the start or framework. Not the book needs so much to be the complete thing, but the reader of the book does. That were to make a nation of supple and athletic minds, well-trained, intuitive, used to depend on themselves, and not on a few coteries of writers.

—Investigating here, we see, not that it is a little thing we have, in having the bequeathed libraries, countless shelves of volumes, records, &c. ; yet how serious the danger, depending entirely on them, of the bloodless vein, the nerveless arm, the false application, at second or third hand. After all, we see Life, not bred, (at least in its more modern and essential parts,) in those great old Libraries, nor America nor Democracy favored nor applauded there. We see that the real interest of this People of ours in the Theology, History, Poetry, Politics, and Personal Models of the past, (the British islands, for instance, and indeed all the past,) is not necessarily to mould ourselves or our literature upon them, but to attain fuller, more definite comparisons, warnings, and the insight to ourselves, our own present, and our own far grander, different, future history, Religion, social customs, &c.

—We see that almost everything that has been written, sung, or stated, of old, with reference to humanity under the Feudal and Oriental institutes, religions, and for other lands, needs to be re-written, resung, re-stated, in terms consistent with the institution of These States, and to come in range and obedient uniformity with them.

We see, as in the universes of the material Kosmos, after meteorological, vegetable, and animal cycles, man at last arises, born through them, to prove them, concentrate them, to turn upon them with wonder and love—to command them, adorn them, and carry them upward into superior realms—so out of the series of the preceding social and political universes, now arise These States—their main purport being not in the newness and importance of their politics or inventions, but in new, grander, more advanced Religions, Literatures, and Art.

We see that while many were supposing things established and completed, really the grandest things always remain ; and discover that the work of the New World is not ended, but only fairly begun.

We see our land, America, her Literature, Esthetics, &c., as, substantially, the getting in form, or effusement and statement, of deepest basic elements and loftiest final meanings, of History and Man—and the portrayal, (under the eternal laws and conditions of beauty,) of our own physiognomy, the subjective tie and expression of the objective, as from our own combination, continuation and points of view—and the deposit and record of the national mentality, character, appeals, heroism, wars, and even liberties—where these, and all, culminate in native formulation, to be perpetuated ;—and not having which native, first-class formulation, she will flounder about, and her other, however imposing, eminent greatness, prove merely a passing gleam ; but truly having which, she will understand herself, live nobly, nobly contribute, emanate, and, swinging, poised

safely on herself, illumined and illuming, become a full-
formed world, and divine Mother not only of material
but spiritual worlds, in ceaseless succession through
Time.

Finally, we have to admit, we see, even to-day, and
in all these things, the born Democratic taste and will
of The United States, regardless of precedent, or of any
authority but their own, beginning to arrive, seeking
place—which, in due time, they will fully occupy. At
first, of course, under current prevalences of theology,
conventions, criticism, &c., all appears impracticable—
takes chances to be denied and misunderstood. There-
with, of course, murmurers, puzzled persons, supercil-
ious inquirers, (with a mighty stir and noise among
these windy little gentlemen that swarm in literature,
in the magazines.) But America, advancing steadily,
evil as well as good, penetrating deep, without one
thought of retraction, ascending, expanding, keeps her
course, hundreds, thousands of years.

GENERAL NOTES.

"Society."—I have myself little or no hope from what is technically called "Society" in our American cities. New York, of which place I have spoken so sharply, still promises something, in time, out of its tremendous and varied materials, with a certain superiority of intuitions, and the advantage of constant agitation, and ever new and rapid dealings of the cards. Of Boston, with its circles of social mummies, swathed in cerements harder than brass—its bloodless religion, (Unitarianism,) its complacent vanity of scientism and literature, lots of grammatical correctness, mere knowledge, (always wearisome, in itself)—its zealous abstractions, ghosts of reforms—I should say, (ever admitting its business powers, its sharp, almost demoniac, intellect, and no lack, in its own way, of courage and generosity)—there is, at present, little of cheering, satisfying sign. In the West, California, &c., "society" is yet unformed, puerile, seemingly unconscious of anything above a driving business, or to liberally spend the money made by it in the usual rounds and shows.

Then there is, to the humorous observer of American attempts at fashion, according to the models of foreign courts and saloons, quite a comic side—particularly visible at Washington City,—a sort of high life below stairs business. As if any farce could be funnier, for instance, than the scenes of the crowds, winter nights, meandering around our Presidents and their wives, Cabinet officers, western or other Senators, Representatives, &c.; born of good laboring, mechanic, or farmer stock and antecedents, attempting those full-dress receptions, finesse of parlors, foreign ceremonies, etiquettes, &c.

Indeed, considered with any sense of propriety, or any sense at all, the whole of this illy-played fashionable play and display, with their absorption of the best part of our wealthier citizens' time, money, energies, &c., is ridiculously out of place in the United States. As if our proper man and woman, (far, far greater words than "gentleman" and "lady,") could still fail to see, and presently achieve, not this spectral business, but something truly noble, active, sane, American—by modes, perfections of character, manners, costumes, social relations, &c., adjusted to standards, far, far different from those!

—Eminent and liberal foreigners, British or continental, must at times have their faith fearfully tried by what they see of our New World personalities. The shallowest and least American persons seem surest to push abroad and call without fail on well-known foreigners, who are doubtless affected with indescribable qualms by these queer ones. Then, more than half of our authors and writers evidently think it a great thing to be "aristocratic," and sneer at progress, democracy, revolution, &c. If some international literary Snobs' Gallery were established, it is certain that America could contribute at least her full share of the portraits, and some very distinguished ones. Observe that the most impudent slanders, low insults, &c., on the great revolutionary authors, leaders, poets, &c., of Europe, have their origin and main circulation in certain circles here. The treatment of Victor Hugo living, and Byron dead, are samples. Both deserving so well of America; and both persistently attempted to be soiled here by unclean birds, male and female.

—Meanwhile, I must still offset the like of the foregoing, and all it infers, by the recognition of the fact, that while the surfaces of current society here show so much that is dismal, noisome and vapory, there are, beyond question, inexhaustible supplies, as of true gold ore, in the mines of America's general humanity. Let us, not ignoring the dross, give fit stress to these precious, immortal values also. Let it be distinctly admitted, that—whatever may be said of our fashionable society, and of any foul fractions and episodes—only here in America, out of the long history, and manifold presentations of the ages, has at last arisen, and now stands, what never before took positive form and sway, THE PEOPLE—and that, viewed en-masse, and while fully acknowledging deficiencies, dangers, faults, this People, inchoate, latent, not yet come to majority, nor to its own religious, literary or esthetic expression, yet affords, to-day, an exultant justification of all the faith, all the hopes and prayers and prophecies of good men through the past—the stablest, solidest-based government of the world—the most assured in a future—the beaming Pharos to whose perennial light all earnest eyes, the world over, are tending—And that already, in and from it, the Democratic principle, having been mortally tried by severest tests, fatalities, of war and peace, now issues from the trial, unharmed, trebly-invigorated, perhaps to commence forthwith its finally triumphant march around the globe.

BRITISH LITERATURE.—To avoid mistake, I would say that I not only commend the study of this literature, but wish our sources of supply and comparison vastly enlarged. American students may well derive from all former lands—from forenoon Greece and Rome, down to the perturbed medieval times, the Crusades, and so to Italy, the German intellect—all the older literatures, and all the newer ones—from witty and warlike France, and markedly, and in many ways, and at many different periods, from the enterprise and soul of the great Spanish race—bearing ourselves always courteous, always deferential, indebted beyond measure to the mother-world, to all its nations dead, as all its nations living—the offspring, this America of ours, the Daughter, not by any means of the British isles exclusively, but of the Continent, and all continents. Indeed, it is time we should realize and fully fructify those germs we also hold from Italy, France, Spain, especially in the best imaginative productions of those lands, which are, in many ways, loftier and subtler than the English, or British, and indispensable to complete our service, proportions, education, reminiscences, &c.....The British element These States hold, and have always held, enormously beyond its fit proportions. I have already spoken of Shakespeare. He seems to me of astral genius, first class, entirely fit for feudalism. His contributions, especially to the literature of the passions, are immense, forever dear to humanity—and his name is always to be reverenced in America. But there is much in him that is offensive to Democracy. He is not only the tally of Feudalism, but I should say Shakespeare is incarnated, uncompromising Feudalism, in literature. Then one seems to detect something in him— I hardly know how to describe it—even amid the dazzle of his genius; and, in inferior manifestations, it is found in nearly all leading British authors. (Perhaps we will have to import the words Snob, Snobbish, &c., after all.) While of the great poems of Asian antiquity, the Indian epics, the Book of Job, the Ionian Iliad, the unsurpassedly simple, loving, perfect idyls of the life and death of Christ, in the New Testament, (indeed Homer and the Biblical utterances intertwine familiarly with us, in the main,) and along down, of most of the characteristic imaginative or romantic relics of the continent, as the Cid, Cervantes' Don Quixote, &c., I should say they substantially adjust themselves to us, and, far off as they are, accord curiously with our bed and board, to-day, in 1870, in Brooklyn, Washington, Canada, Ohio, Texas, California—and with our notions, both of seriousness and of fun, and our standards of heroism, manliness, and even the Democratic requirements—those requirements are not only not fulfilled in the Shakesperean productions, but are insulted on every page.

I add that—while England is among the greatest of lands in political freedom, or the idea of it, and in stalwart personal character, &c.—the spirit of English literature is not great, at least is not greatest—and its products are no models for us. With the exception of Shakespeare, there is no first-class genius, or approaching to first-class, in that literature—which, with a truly vast amount of value, and of artificial beauty, (largely from the classics,) is almost always material, sensual, not spiritual—almost always congests, makes plethoric, not frees, expands, dilates—is cold, anti-Democratic, loves to be sluggish and stately, and shows much of that characteristic of vulgar persons, the dread of saying or doing something not at all improper in itself, but unconventional, and that may be laughed at. In its best, the sombre per-

vades it;—it is moody, melancholy, and, to give it its due, expresses, in characters and plots, those qualities, in an unrivaled
manner. Yet not as the black thunderstorms, and in great normal, crashing passions, as of the Greek dramatists—clearing the
air, refreshing afterward, bracing with power; but as in Hamlet,
moping, sick, uncertain, and leaving ever after a secret taste for
the blues, the morbid fascination, the luxury of wo.....(I cannot
dismiss English, or British imaginative literature without the
cheerful name of Walter Scott. In my opinion he deserves to
stand next to Shakespeare. Both are, in their best and absolute
quality, continental, not British—both teeming, luxuriant, true to
their lands and origin, namely feudality, yet ascending into universalism. Then, I should say, both deserve to be finally considered and construed as shining suns, whom it were ungracious to
pick spots upon.)

I strongly recommend all the young men and young women of
the United States to whom it may be eligible, to overhaul the
well-freighted fleets, the literatures of Italy, Spain, France, Germany, so full of those elements of freedom, self-possession, gay-
heartedness, subtlety, dilation, needed in preparations for the
future of The States. I only wish we could have really good
translations. I rejoice at the feeling for Oriental researches and
poetry, and hope it will go on.

THE LATE WAR.—The Secession War in the United States
appears to me as the last great material and military outcropping
of the Feudal spirit, in our New World history, society, &c.
Though it was not certain, hardly probable, that the effort for
founding a Slave-Holding power, by breaking up the Union,
should be successful, it was urged on by indomitable passion,
pride and will. The signal downfall of this effort, the abolition
of Slavery, and the extirpation of the Slaveholding Class, (cut
out and thrown away like a tumor by surgical operation,) makes
incomparably the longest advance for Radical Democracy, utterly
removing its only really dangerous impediment, and insuring its
progress in the United States—and thence, of course, over the
world.....(Our immediate years witness the solution of three vast,
life-threatening calculi, in different parts of the world—the removal
of serfdom in Russia, slavery in the United States, and of the
meanest of Imperialisms in France.)

Of the Secession War itself, we know, in the ostent, what has
been done. The numbers of the dead and wounded can be told,
or approximated, the debt posted and put on record, the material
events narrated, &c. Meantime, the war being over, elections go
on, laws are passed, political parties struggle, issue their platforms, &c., just the same as before. But immensest results of the
War—not only in Politics, but in Literature, Poems, and Sociology—are doubtless waiting yet unformed, in the future. How
long they will wait I cannot tell. The pageant of History's
retrospect shows us, ages since, all Europe marching on the Cru-

sades, those wondrous armed uprisings of the People, stirred by a mere idea, to grandest attempt—and, when once baffled in it, returning, at intervals, twice, thrice, and again. An unsurpassed series of revolutionary events, influences. Yet it took over two hundred years for the seeds of the Crusades to germinate before beginning even to sprout. Two hundred years they lay, sleeping, not dead, but dormant in the ground. Then, out of them, unerringly, arts, travel, navigation, politics, literature, freedom, inventions, the spirit of adventure, inquiry, all arose, grew, and steadily sped on to what we see at present. Far back there, that huge agitation-struggle of the Crusades, stands, as undoubtedly the embryo, the start, of the high preëminence of experiment, civilization and enterprise which the European nations have since sustained, and of which These States are the heirs.

GENERAL SUFFRAGE, ELECTIONS, &c.—It still remains doubtful to me whether these will ever secure, officially, the best wit and capacity—whether, through them, the first-class genius of America will ever personally appear in the high political stations, the Presidency, Congress, the leading State offices, &c. Those offices, or the candidacy for them, arranged, won, by caucusing, money, the favoritism or pecuniary interest of rings, the superior manipulation of the ins over the outs, or the outs over the ins, are, indeed, at best, the mere business agencies of the people, are useful as formulating, neither the best and highest, but the average of the public judgment, sense, justice, (or sometimes want of judgment, sense, justice.) We elect Presidents, Congressmen, &c., not so much to have them consider and decide for us, but as surest practical means of expressing the will of majorities on mooted questions, measures, &c.

As to general suffrage, after all, since we have gone so far, the more general it is, the better. I favor the widest opening of the doors. Let the ventilation and area be wide enough, and all is safe. We can never have a born penitentiary-bird, or panel-thief, or lowest gambling-hell or groggery keeper, for President—though such may not only emulate, but get, high offices from localities— even from the proud and wealthy city of New York.

STATE RIGHTS.—Freedom, (under the universal laws,) and the fair and uncramped play of Individuality, can only be had at all through strong-knit cohesion, identity. There are, who, talking of the rights of The States, as in separatism and independence, condemn a rigid nationality, centrality. But to my mind, the freedom, as the existence at all, of The States, pre-necessitates such a Nationality, an imperial Union. Thus, it is to serve separatism that we favor generalization, consolid on. It is to give, under the compaction of potent general law, an independent vitality and sway within their spheres, to The States singly, (really just as important a part of our scheme as the sacred Union itself,) that we insist on the preservation of our Nationality forever, and at all hazards. I say neither States, nor any thing like State Rights, could permanently exist on any other terms.

LATEST FROM EUROPE.—As I send my last pages to press, (Sept. 19, 1870,) the ocean-cable, continuing its daily budget of Franco-German war-news—Louis Napoleon a prisoner, (his rat-cunning at an end)—the conquerors advanced on Paris—the French, assuming Republican forms—seeking to negotiate with the King of Prussia, at the head of his armies—"his Majesty," says the despatch, "refuses to treat, on any terms, with a govern-ment risen out of Democracy."

Let us note the words, and not forget them. The official rela-tions of Our States, we know, are with the reigning kings, queens, &c., of the Old World. But the only deep, vast, emotional, real affinity of America is with the cause of Popular Government there—and especially in France. O that I could express, in my printed lines, the passionate yearnings, the pulses of sympathy, forever throbbing in the heart of These States, for sake of that—the eager eyes forever turned to that—watching it, struggling, appearing and disappearing, often apparently gone under, yet never to be abandoned, in France, Italy, Spain, Germany, and in the British Islands.

{ Annotations for *Democratic Vistas* }

Full publication information is given for criticism cited in the notes, except for criticism that is included in the "Selected Bibliography of Works about *Democratic Vistas*," where full publication information is provided. Abbreviations of cited works by Whitman can be found on page ix at the front of this book.

Whitman originally intended to include section subtitles throughout *Democratic Vistas*, but as the work went to press, the subtitles were cancelled. They are offered here for the convenience of the reader and for general interest (followed by the page number on which, and beginning of the paragraph before which, the subtitle was intended to appear):

Our Real Grandeur Abroad. (3: "America, filling the present")

I Admit Democracy's Dangers. (3: "But let me strike")

American Arts, Poems, Theology. (5: "I say that Democracy")

The Main Organ and Medium. (6: "Viewed, to-day,")

New World Ideas — Representers. (9: "I suggest, therefore,")

The Gravest Question of All. (11: "For my part,")

Individualism Versus the Aggregate. (15: "And now, in the full conception")

The War Proved Democracy. (19: "The movements of the late Secession war,")

Consideration — Customs — Law — the Esthetic — Cohesion. (21: "Meantime,")

Our Lesson to Europe. (24: "A portion of our pages")

Reformers, Money-Makers, &c. (26: "The eager")

Indefiniteness in 1868. (27: "— Huge and mighty")

Evil Also Serves. (29: "— Once, before the war,")

A Thought in My Musings. (31: "Then still the thought returns,")

Page 3

AMERICA, filling the present

> When Whitman reprinted *Democratic Vistas* in his
> *Specimen Days and Collect* (1882), he added a new

opening paragraph to precede the original one: "As the greatest lessons of Nature through the universe are perhaps the lessons of variety and freedom, the same present the greatest lessons also in New World politics and progress. If a man were ask'd, for instance, the distinctive points contrasting modern European and American political and other life with the old Asiatic cultus, as lingering-bequeath'd yet in China and Turkey, he might find the amount of them in John Stuart Mill's profound essay on Liberty in the future, where he demands two main constituents, or sub-strata, for a truly grand nationality—1st, a large variety of character— and 2nd, full play for human nature to expand itself in numberless and even conflicting directions—(seems to be for general humanity much like the influences that make up, in their limitless field, that perennial health-action of the air we call the weather—an infinite number of currents and forces, and contributions, and temperatures, and cross purposes, whose ceaseless play of counterpart upon counterpart brings constant restoration and vitality.) With this thought—and not for itself along, but all necessitates, and draws after it—let me begin my speculations." Whitman here invokes English philosopher John Stuart Mill's 1859 essay "On Liberty," in which Mill probed the same tension that concerns Whitman in *Democratic Vistas*—the relationship between society and the individual. In examining the tension between authority and liberty, Mill argued for a radically expanded individual liberty: "The only freedom which deserves the name is that of pursuing our own good in our own way, so long as we do not attempt to deprive others, or impede their efforts to obtain it. . . . Mankind are greater gainers by suffering each other to live as seems good to themselves, than by compelling each to live as seems good to the rest." Whitman agrees with Mill that it is crucial to have an unregimented society that encourages diversity of activity and thought. Mill wrote that people, if they were to be truly human, could not live their lives in "ape-like imitation" of prescribed models of behavior, and so Whitman contrasts the emerging democracies of Europe and America with the "old Asiatic cultus," organized forms of worship and behavior-control that bred conformity. Mill in his essay warned that England was in danger of "advancing towards the Chinese ideal of making all people alike," and Whitman endorses this view that China and Turkey are examples of what Mill called "making a people all alike, . . . governing their thoughts and conduct by the same maxims and rules."

Feudalism

Whitman frequently used the notion of feudalism as a contrast to his vision of democracy. Whereas feudalism represented the past and, often, European traditions for Whitman, democracy was the present and, even more, the future of the United States. And whereas, for Whitman, feudalism was a system of aristocracy supported by the labor of the masses, democracy was a system of equality, self-realization, and the common man.

kosmos

In his poem "Kosmos," Whitman includes in his concept of the kosmos, or natural order, not only the earth and Nature but also human beings. One of the roles of the Poet is, for Whitman, bringing humans into unity with this cosmic order. Whitman maintains the German spelling of "kosmos," a term he picked up from Prussian naturalist Alexander von Humboldt's five-volume *Kosmos* (1845–1850), a work that influenced him greatly in its exploration of how the material universe was a complex but ordered system, "animated by the breath of life," that might help him reconceive of identity itself.

the Democratic Republican principle,
and the theory of development and perfection
by voluntary standards, and self-suppliance

> Whitman struggles in this essay with the problems of
> democracy in practice as a tug-of-war between the many
> and the one. Here he emphasizes individual freedoms
> (voluntary improvement and "self-suppliance"), but puts
> them in service of the larger ideal of democracy. Ralph
> Waldo Emerson's essay "Self-Reliance" was published
> in 1841, and Whitman was influenced by Emerson's
> argument that we must rely on the truth that we have in
> ourselves rather than on an outside interpreter or leader.
> This Self, however, is universal, existing in all others
> (what the Transcendentalists called the "oversoul").
> Whitman's notion of self-reliance here echoes Emerson's
> in the sense that it is both individual and universal, but
> his use of the term "self-suppliance" indicates how he
> was often trying to distance himself from Emerson, even
> while inevitably echoing him. In later reprintings of
> *Democratic Vistas*, Whitman abandoned the clumsy "self-
> suppliance" and replaced it with Emerson's more elegant
> "self-reliance."

Page 4

these stirring years of war and peace

> Whitman wrote *Democratic Vistas* in 1867–1870,
> the chaotic years of "peace," when the United States
> underwent Reconstruction following the chaotic years of
> the Civil War (1861–1865). Both periods were "stirring" for
> Whitman because he sensed great changes occurring in
> the nation, changes he believed would ultimately be for
> the good.

the appalling dangers of universal suffrage

> In 1869 the Fifteenth Amendment gave all males the
> right to vote; that same year, women won voting rights in

Wyoming. Whitman was a supporter of universal suffrage, but he also conceded that universal suffrage in Europe would cause problems because European paupers were poorly educated. Here Whitman suggests that suffrage alone will not create equality but that the vote must go hand-in-hand with a program of improvement.

[fn] *density of Belgium's population*

Belgium is 11,873 square miles in size and had a population, in 1868, of 4,961,644 inhabitants, according to the *American Annual Cyclopedia and Register of Important Events*, 1871; its population density would have been 418 people per square mile. Vice President Schuyler Colfax was President Ulysses Grant's vice president from 1868 to 1873. He was a well-known, much beloved, and very successful lecturer, known for his patriotic and stirring Fourth of July speeches, from one of which Whitman takes this quotation.

Page 5

the Ecclesiastic traditions, though palpably retreating from political institutions

While Whitman saw religion as important to the self-improvement that is necessary for democracy, he felt that churches tended to tamp down individualism by preventing people from thinking for themselves. Rather than being led by ministers of particular faiths, individuals must, Whitman felt, understand religion and morality on their own terms. In 1842 when Catholic schools sought the support of public funds, Whitman, as editor of the *Aurora*, criticized what he saw as the teaching of religion in public schools in defiance of the basic democratic principle of the separation of church and state. By the 1860s, however, Whitman expressed some admiration for formalized religion, even though he himself never subscribed to any particular creed.

tariff

One of the contributing causes of the Civil War was tariffs, or taxes paid on goods imported to the United States. The manufacturing North saw the agricultural South presented as a wealthy market that they were losing to cheaper imports, so the North supported import tariffs to protect their market. The South felt that import tariffs targeted them unfairly because they purchased more imported goods than the North. After the Civil War, Congress imposed even higher import tariffs in order to raise money to pay off the public debt.

labor questions

During Whitman's lifetime, the class of skilled artisans into which he was born was slowly transformed into a class of largely unskilled, wage-earning laborers and small-scale entrepreneurs. He was a fervent supporter of labor interests on such issues as labor conditions and exploitation, monopolies, paper money and banking, and temperance. Despite Whitman's hopes that returning Civil War soldiers would create a new republic of artisans, post-Civil War America instead quickly became a modern and fiercely competitive industrialized economy, which led to bitter class struggles. (M. Wynn Thomas, "Labor and Laboring Classes" in *WWE*, 344–345)

Page 6

Literatuses

Whereas "literati" refers to the educated classes, the intelligentsia, Whitman uses the term "literatuses" here to refer to a kind of priestly class that can speak to the common people. This is one of the contradictions of Whitman's vision of democracy: though he believes in a society of equals, he also believes that a class of elites is required to educate and guide the people. Whitman pluralizes "literatus" using the standard English way of creating plurals (as "literatuses" instead of the Latin plural "literati," with its connotation of aristocratic snobbery), and he thus coins a new word that makes his paradoxically democratic/elite group sound more American.

the people of our land may all know how to read and write

In 1870 the literacy rate in America was 80 percent. However, of the 20 percent of the population that was illiterate, over 90 percent were in the bottom half of the income bracket, and illiteracy was largest in the population of immigrant women.

Page 7

Judah

The Biblical Kingdom of Judah (or Hebrew Tribe) produced a rich literary tradition. (Judah refers both to the united Kingdom of Judah, including Israel, and to the separate Kingdom of Judah, also known as the Southern Kingdom after its split from the Kingdom of Israel, but Whitman is likely referring to both here, encompassing the period from 1030 BC to 586 BC.)

ostent

The 1876 Webster's defines ostent as (1) appearance; air; manner; mien; (2) show; manifestation; token; (3) a portent; any thing ominous. In more recent philosophy, ostension refers to the most primitive form of signification, the act of showing objects and events (rather than, for example, describing them). Whitman's usage seems to tend in the direction of this more contemporary meaning; he suggests that wars, uprisings, and other plays of power overtly and easily demonstrate their influence, but these are primitive forms of influence, less far-reaching than new thoughts, principles, literary style, and imagination.

[fn] *hereditaments*

According to the 1876 Webster's, hereditament is

"any species of property that may be inherited; lands, tenements, any thing corporeal or incorporeal, real, personal, or mixed, that may descend to an heir." It goes on to note that "A corporeal hereditament is visible and tangible; an incorporeal hereditament is an ideal right, existing in contemplation of a law, issuing out of substantial corporeal property." Interestingly, Whitman's usage here seems to combine the corporeal and incorporeal in his description of various poetic traditions as contributing to the "osseous [or skeletal] structure [of European chivalry and feudalism] . . . preserving its flesh and bloom, giving it form . . . saturating it in the conscious and unconscious blood, breed, belief, and intuitions of men" (957).

[fn] *Walter Scott's Border Minstrelsy*

Minstrelsy of the Scottish Border: consisting of historical and romantic ballads, collected in the Southern Counties of Scotland; with a few of modern date, founded upon local tradition was an anthology of Scottish ballads published by Walter Scott in 1802.

[fn] *Percy's Collection*

Thomas Percy's *Reliques of Ancient English Poetry* (1765), an anthology of ancient ballads.

[fn] *Ellis's Early English Metrical Romances*

George Ellis's *Specimens of Early English Metrical Romances, Chiefly Written During the Early Part of the Fourteenth Century; To Which is Prefixed An Historical Introduction, Intended to Illustrate the Rise and Progress of Romantic Composition in France and England*, published in 1805.

[fn] *the European Continental Poems of Walter of Aquitania, and the Nibelungen*

The Nibelungen is a literary tradition of medieval German heroes, one of whom was Walter of Aquitania, also known as Walter of Spain and Waltari af Waskastein.

[fn] *the history of the Troubadours, by Fauriel*
  Histoire de la poesie provençale by Claude-Charles
  Fauriel, published in 1846.

[fn] *old Hindu epics*

The Ramayana and the Mahabharata, the two most
important ancient epics of India, containing the teachings of Hindu sages, were written around the fourth
century BC. Parts of both epics began to be translated
into English early in the nineteenth century, and more
of the epics became accessible in English throughout
Whitman's lifetime.

[fn] *Ticknor's chapters on the Cid, and on the*
Spanish poems and poets of Calderon's time

George Ticknor's three-volume *History of Spanish
Literature*, published in 1864.

[fn] *the Shakspearean dramas*

The English playwright William Shakespeare produced
most of his known works between 1590 and 1613.

Page 9

[Greece's] sad unity of a common subjection,
at the last, to foreign conquerors

Ancient Greece is often seen as the founder of Western
civilization, and its influence stretched from at least
1100 BC until its defeat by Roman conquerors in 146 BC.

Page 11

the Union just issued, victorious

The American Civil War ended on April 9, 1865, when
the Confederate commander Robert E. Lee surrendered
to Union commander Ulysses S. Grant at Appomattox,
Virginia.

the vertebrae, to State or man

Whitman here begins his comparison of the human
body to the "body politic," noting how both individual

humans and the state itself must have backbone, a basic structure (here, "moral conscience") to support the entire body. Note how throughout the essay, physical images (e.g., "dyspeptic," "eructations," "morbific," "scrofulous," "cankerous," "abnormal libidinousness," "marrow," "osseous structure") come to represent the nation, as in the next note.

like a physician diagnosing some deep disease

Whitman was always interested in the body, and his poetry is filled with bodily imagery. That imagery continues to be important in this essay, where the body has become America's "body politic," which is now diseased by the corruptions Whitman catalogs here.

Conversation is a mass of badinage

"Badinage" is a French term for light, playful, often silly banter; Whitman's ironic use of the French term here indicates his scorn for the tendency of people to artificially inflate their conversation (as he himself often does with his use of French terms like "badinage").

An acute and candid person, in the
Revenue Department in Washington

Charles W. Eldridge, one of the publishers of Whitman's 1860–61 *Leaves of Grass*, worked in the late 1860s in the Internal Revenue Department in Washington. He and Whitman and another author and government worker, William Douglas O'Connor, met almost nightly to discuss the issues of the day.

Page 12

The magician's serpent in the fable ate up all the other serpents

This may be a reference to the Biblical story of Aaron's rod, in which Moses's brother Aaron carried, during the plagues that preceded the Exodus, a rod endowed with miraculous power. The story that Whitman recalls here is, however, different from the Biblical account. In the Exodus story, Aaron's rod becomes a serpent which swallows up the serpents of the Egyptian Pharaoh's magicians—a warning to the Pharaoh not to resist God's power. Whitman's confusion over the owner of the rod (he calls it the "magician's serpent") suggests that Whitman sees the rod—here equated with the capitalist drive to make money—as an evil master, swallowing up everything around it. Whitman's critique of the modern industrial nation the United States has become is pointed, and he repeats again and again in this essay his condemnation of showy wealth and unnecessary extravagance at the expense of the laboring masses.

beyond Alexander's [empire]

Alexander the Great (356 BC–323 BC), King of Macedon, conquered the Persian Empire and, adding it to his European territories, ruled what was presumed to be most of the world as known to the ancient Greeks.

beyond the proudest sway of Rome

At the height of its power, around AD 150, Rome controlled the entire western world as known at the time, an area stretching from Britain and Germany to North Africa and the Persian Gulf.

annex Texas, California, Alaska, and reach
north for Canada and south for Cuba

The Republic of Texas was voluntarily annexed as the twenty-eighth state in 1845; California, ceded to the United States in the Mexican Cession of 1848, became the thirty-first state in 1850; Alaska was purchased from Russia in 1867 (the Alaska Purchase is also known as Seward's Folly), but Alaska did not become the forty-ninth state until 1959. In the nineteenth century, during the height of America's sense of its "manifest destiny" to eventually occupy the entire continent, many Americans (like John L. O'Sullivan, who in 1845 coined the phrase "manifest destiny") assumed that eventually Canada and

Cuba would become part of the United States, either
by conquest or consent. Whitman's view was that there
was a kind of inevitable force of democracy that would
eventually embrace other countries, creating an "America"
that was larger than the "United States," a kind of
irresistible international nationalism that did not involve
conquest.

I am now (September, 1870,) again in
New York City and Brooklyn

Whitman lived in Brooklyn for nearly thirty years, longer
than any place else. He moved with his family to Brooklyn
from Long Island on May 27, 1823, just before his fourth
birthday. The Brooklyn Whitman originally moved to
was rural, but by the time of the Civil War it was the
third largest city in the United States, and by 1870 it had
a population of nearly four hundred thousand, still less
than half of that of New York, the nation's largest city,
which was then nearing a million. Whitman lived in New
York City as a teenager and spent a lot of time there,
traveling back and forth by ferry from Brooklyn, until he
took up residency in Washington in 1863. He was in New
York and Brooklyn for three months in the fall of 1870,
during which time he arranged for the publication of
Democratic Vistas, on which he was still working, making
changes and additions, as usual, up to the last minute, as
he indicates here.

Page 13
Broadway

This was one of Whitman's favorite streets in his
favorite city of New York. In his poem "Broadway,"
Whitman writes "What hurrying human tides, or day
or night! / What passions, winnings, losses, ardors,
swim thy waters! / What whirls of evil, bliss and sorrow,
stem thee!" Broadway, for Whitman, represented the

movement and fullness of crowds of citizens assembling for all different purposes.

jobbers' houses

In 1870 usage, jobbers' houses could be stockbrokers' offices or importers' offices.

Central Park, and the Brooklyn Park of Hills

Central Park in New York City and Prospect Park in Brooklyn were both designed by Frederick Law Olmstead and Calvert Vaux, innovators in the development of urban parks. (Before the creation of city parks, urban citizens used cemeteries as the places to escape to nature.) Central Park (over eight hundred acres) was not so central when it was planned in the late 1850s, but Olmstead and Vaux projected that the city would grow around the park and thus eventually make it a tranquil oasis in the vast metropolis that was developing around it. They designed Prospect Park just after the Civil War. Both parks officially opened in 1873, so when Whitman wrote *Democratic Vistas*, the parks were still under construction, but already thousands of people were using them. Both parks required massive reconstruction of the natural environments. Prospect Park (nearly six hundred acres) featured a hilly landscape which provided inspiring views and thus was for Whitman a "Park of Hills."

Wall street, or the gold exchange

Wall Street, in lower Manhattan, was from the late eighteenth century a center for trading and finance. The Gold Exchange was opened in Wall Street in 1864, the result of a wild speculation in gold brought on by the Union's issuing of greenbacks (paper money) during the war. Depending on the day-to-day fortunes of the Union army, gold prices fluctuated tremendously as investors worried that Union greenbacks would collapse as a currency if the Union lost the war. The year before Whitman "passed an hour" in the hectic Gold Exchange, it was the site of "Black Friday," one of the great financial panics in American history, as two speculators, James Fisk and Jay Gould, tried to corner the gold market with the help of President Ulysses Grant's brother-in-law. Grant's reputation suffered in 1870 because of the scandal, the first of several during his two terms as president.

Page 15

[fn] *modern Individualism*

Individualism, or what Whitman also referred to as Personalism, puts the individual person at the center of all considerations of human rights, liberty, and morality. Although Whitman's ultimate vision was of a democracy of individuals coming together for the collective good—a delicate balance between the needs and interests of the individual and the needs and interests of the collective—here he attests to the conflict between the two as a source of social unrest. As Garyl Wihl argues, Whitman's arguments about Individualism draw upon "the liberal debates of his time, but frames these debates in the language of romantic recollection, sentiment, and imaginative vision" ("Politics," *A Companion to Walt Whitman*, ed. Donald D. Kummings [Malden, Massachusetts: Blackwell, 2006], 76), and literary culture becomes for Whitman a way of reconciling the individual with the collective.

Page 16

1790

This is the year that the American government fully began operating after its revolutionary beginnings, as Rhode Island became the last of the original thirteen states to ratify the Constitution. President Washington, elected the previous year, gave the first State of the Union address;

the Supreme Court met for the first time; the White
House began to be built. There were a number of "long
slumbering" "eructations" [violent eruptions] occurring
that year: the French Revolution, which had begun the
year before, gained full force in 1790, when the National
Assembly abolished nobility, and the French Revolution
prompted the successful slave uprising in Haiti (then a
French colony known as Saint-Dominque) that began
in earnest in 1791 and drove whites out by 1803; in 1790
the free people of color in Haiti began the revolt when
they were denied the right to vote by the French colonial
governor.

Page 18
"THE GOVERNMENT OF THE PEOPLE,
BY THE PEOPLE, FOR THE PEOPLE"

From Abraham Lincoln's most famous speech, the
Gettysburg Address, delivered on November 19, 1863.
In it Lincoln envisions that the nation, divided by civil
war, would ultimately be reunited in liberty. His famous
phrase here is a memorable articulation of the idea that
democracy rests on the consent of the governed, an
important principle at the time Whitman was writing
Democratic Vistas, when the discussion over whether
freed slaves and women had the right to vote struck at the
very heart of who the "governed" were and how, if they
could not vote, they were to give their "consent."

[fn] *"Shooting Niagara"*

Whitman wrote what ultimately became *Democratic
Vistas* in response to the Scottish essayist Thomas
Carlyle's "Shooting Niagara: And After?" first appearing
in the United States in the *New York Tribune* (August 16,
1867). See the introduction for a full discussion of this
essay and Whitman's response to Carlyle.

Page 19
haut ton coteries

> Whitman turns to the French language to capture
> the tone of the aristocratic classes, the high-toned,
> high-fashion set who stand in stark contrast to the
> "ungrammatical, untidy . . . and ill-bred" mass of "The
> People" that Whitman celebrates here as the great subject
> for a new democratic literature. When Whitman wrote
> this, France was still ruled by the emperor Napoleon III
> and had a strongly delineated class system.

American-born populace

> Here Whitman argues that America needs to be free of
> foreign influences, which is why he especially looks to
> Americans born on American soil. This is a different
> stance from that of the Native American Party, who in the
> 1840s and 1850s rallied for strict limits on immigration,
> especially for Irish Catholics, and for restricting eligibility
> for public office to "native born Americans," i.e., non-
> immigrants. Although Whitman also wanted America
> to be independent, he criticized the Native American
> Party as anti-foreigner; he himself wished to exclude no
> one from the benefits of freedom and democracy that
> America represented. (For Whitman's critique of the
> Native American Party, see his 1842 newspaper article
> "Americanism": "Yet with all our antipathy for every
> thing that may tend to assimilate our country to the
> kingdoms of Europe, we repudiate such doctrines as
> have characterised the 'Native American' party. We
> would see no man disfranchised, because he happened
> to be born three thousand miles off. . . . Let us receive
> these foreigners to our shores, and to our good offices"
> [*J* 1:124–125].)

Page 20

Fredericksburg

> The Battle of Fredericksburg, Virginia (December 11–15,
> 1862), resulted in staggering casualties and overwhelm-
> ing defeat for the Union army. According to National
> Park Service estimates, the Union army casualties
> rose above thirteen thousand, while Confederate army
> casualties were roughly 4,500. This is the battle in which
> Whitman's brother George was injured, resulting in
> Whitman's going to Fredericksburg to nurse him; once
> he saw the injured soldiers and accompanied them back
> to Washington, D.C., hospitals, he decided to stay in the
> capital and devote himself to aiding the wounded soldiers
> there.

Wilderness

> The battle of Wilderness, fought in central Virginia
> (May 5–7, 1864), resulted in severe casualties for both
> sides. Casualty estimates from the National Park Service
> are 18,400 for the Union army and over 11,400 for the
> Confederate army.

Gettysburg

> The Battle of Gettysburg, Pennsylvania, took place July
> 1–3, 1863, and resulted in the greatest number of
> casualties of the Civil War—twenty-three thousand
> for the Union and twenty-eight thousand for the
> Confederacy, by National Park Service estimates. It is
> considered by many to be the turning point of the war.

America have we seen, though only in her
early youth, already to hospital brought

> This image of the war bringing the entire nation to a
> hospital was a familiar one to Whitman, who spent the
> last two years of the war visiting soldiers in the more
> than fifty hospitals that had sprung up in and around the
> nation's capital. Whitman first used this phrase in a letter
> to Ralph Waldo Emerson in January of 1863: "I desire and

intend to write a little book out of this phase of America, her masculine young manhood, its conduct under most trying of an highest of all exigency, which she, as by lifting a corner in a curtain, has vouchsafed me to see America, already brought to Hospital in her fair youth—brought and deposited here in this great, whited sepulchre of Washington itself" (*C* 1:69). The "little book" Whitman refers to in this letter may suggest his very first imagining of what would come to be *Democratic Vistas*.

Page 21

what I learned personally mixing in such scenes

From 1862 to 1865, during the Civil War, Whitman served as an untrained nurse, a visitor to the many makeshift Civil War hospitals, taking care of wounded and dying soldiers almost daily. He talked with them, read books and newspapers to them, gave them candy and other treats, and wrote letters home for them as they dictated what they wanted to say. Whitman's work in the hospital also made him a source of news for families, friends, and fellow soldiers looking for information about loved ones, and Whitman's wartime letters reveal that he was much appreciated in this capacity.

Patent Office Hospital in Washington City

In January 1863, Whitman volunteered in the hospitals in and around Washington, D.C., including the U.S. Patent Office, which (like a number of government buildings) had been turned into a hospital. The month before, the Union army had suffered staggering casualties at Fredericksburg, Virginia. In the converted Patent Office building, Whitman noted the irony of the rows of sick, badly wounded, and dying soldiers surrounding the glass cases displaying American inventions—guns and machines and other signs of progress. The wrecked bodies dispersed among the displays were what "progress" had brought, the result of the new inventions that had created modern warfare.

Bull Run

The First Battle of Bull Run (known by the Confederates as the First Battle of Manassas), fought on July 21, 1861, near Manassas, Virginia, was the Civil War's first major land battle.

Antietam

The Battle of Antietam (frequently known in the South as the Battle of Sharpsburg) was fought on September 17, 1862, near Sharpsburg, Maryland. It was the first major battle of the Civil War to be fought in the North; it is also the bloodiest single-day battle in U.S. history, with 23,100 total casualties (National Parks Service).

Page 26

There is (turning home again,)

Whitman omitted this paragraph when he republished *Democratic Vistas* in *Specimen Days and Collect* (1882). It is a remarkable statement about how the "thought of Oneness" is the "twin-sister" of America's "Democracy," so intertwined that if one dies, the other lives on only by "dragging a corpse" with it forever. Just as the thought of the promised Messiah guided and inspired "the ancient race of Israel" through its stormy long history, so will this thought of Oneness guide America, continually, "averaging, including all," leveling the people, flattening out class difference, undoing hierarchy, assuring equality of citizens and states, preserving the "sacred Union of These States." This paragraph, written in the years following the Civil War (a war Whitman often referred to as the War to Preserve the Union), reflects Whitman's fervent desire to see the Union restored and reconciled in the later 1860s. This idea of a single Identity, he believed, will guide and preserve the nation through peace and war, and it will not be undone by either the "scalding blood of war" (as the United States had just experienced) or the "rotted ichor of peace" (as the nation was now experiencing). "Ichor" is defined in the 1876 Webster's as "a thin, watery humor" or a "colorless matter flowing from an ulcer"; it is also the ethereal substance that ran in the veins of Greek gods instead of blood. As Whitman makes clear in *Democratic Vistas*, peacetime can bring its own corruptions and can present dangers to the nation every bit as severe as war; thus his imagery of bodily disease as he looks at America "like a physician diagnosing some deep disease." Whitman examines plenty of ulcers that have appeared on the formerly healthy body of his country.

Page 27

As I write this passage, (November, 1868,)
the din of disputation rages around me

The presidential election of November 3, 1868, was the first to take place during Reconstruction (though Texas, Mississippi, and Virginia were not allowed to vote in the election because they had not yet been readmitted to the Union). The election's most hotly debated issue was Reconstruction, which concerned the South's reintroduction back into the Union and the status of freed slaves. The Democratic nominee Horatio Seymour advocated peaceful reconciliation between the North and the South. Republican nominee Ulysses S. Grant, the popular Civil War general, supported more radical reconstruction, black suffrage, and military enforcement of Reconstruction policies, including the passage of the Fourteenth Amendment to the Constitution (ratified on July 9, 1868), which granted citizenship, including the right to equal protection and to due process, to all native-born and naturalized Americans, including freed slaves. Grant won the election by 6 percent of the popular vote. Whitman had hopes that Grant, despite his Republican leanings, would be a moderating force in checking the social upheaval of the postwar years; in February of 1868, Whitman had written in a letter, "The Republicans have exploited the negro too intensely, & there comes a reaction. But that is going to be provided for. According to present appearances the good, worthy, non-demonstrative, average-representing Grant will be chosen President next fall" (*C* 2:15).

Page 28

twenty-first Presidentiad

Horace Traubel recalls Whitman's efforts to get his coinage—"Presidentiad"—added to the dictionary and his explanation of the term: "Its allusion, the four years of the Presidency: its origin that of the Olympiad—but as I flatter myself, bravely appropriate, where not another one word, signifying the same thing, exists!" (*WWWC* 194). Whitman's coinage provides a word for every four-year term of the presidency, so a president who serves two full terms takes up two presidentiads; a president who dies in office shares a presidentiad with the vice president who fills out his term. The twenty-first presidentiad, then, refers to the 1868 election of Grant and his first term in office (1869–1873); there had been twenty four-year presidential terms (presidentiads) before his election. Like the Olympiad, the Presidentiad is a four-year period between contested events.

Our future National Capital may
not be where the present one is

Whitman's argument here that "the dominion-heart of America will be far inland" and that "the main social, political spine-character of The States will probably run along the Ohio, Missouri and Mississippi Rivers" was part of a nationwide controversy in the post-Civil War years about whether the nation's capital should be moved to the Midwest in order to reflect the changing geographical spread of the country. In the logic of Whitman's nation/body imagery, if the heart and spine of the United States are in the Midwest, then the capital should be too. The December 1869 *Western Monthly*, a Chicago magazine, ran a controversial article called "Should the Capitol Be Removed?" reporting on a meeting in St. Louis of delegates from sixteen Western states and territories who argued that the nation now needed to be realigned politically from North/South to East/West, and that the capital needed to be "removed" to the Mississippi Valley. During the various state constitutional conventions called to ratify the Fifteenth Amendment in 1869, a number of Midwestern states petitioned unsuccessfully for the relocation of the capital. Mark Twain, born and raised in the Midwest, captured the futility of the relocation movement by noting in 1869, "It is agitated *every* year. It always has been, it always will be" (*Mark Twain's Letters*, vol. 3, ed. Victor Fisher and Michael B. Frank [Berkeley: University of California Press, 1992], 310).

Page 30

scalliwags

A derisive term for white Southerners who supported Reconstruction after the Civil War, often for their own personal gain. In the 1876 Webster's, "scalawag" was a vulgar term for a miserable tramp.

supple-jacks

A supple-jack is a climbing shrub native to the Southern United States, noted for being both tough and pliable. It is also a term for "a child's toy, a jointed manikin worked by a string," also known as a "Jumping Jack" (John Russell Bartlett, *Dictionary of Americanisms*, 2nd ed. [Boston:

Little, Brown, 1859]). Whitman is clearly using the term in this way, indicating how common American citizens become the puppets of maneuvering politicians, just as corrupt political parties are using the U.S. government itself as a kind of supple-jack, manipulating it to do their bidding.

Page 33

Did you, too, O friend, suppose Democracy
was only for elections, for politics

In this paragraph, Whitman makes some of his most radical claims, proposing that democracy is not just or even primarily a form of governance but a way of life, as he imagines the eventual democratization of all aspects of social interaction, from religion through education through even the military—ultimately "democracy in all public and private life."

[fn] *present system of the officering and personnel of the Army and Navy of These States, and the spirit and letter of their trebly-aristocratic rules and regulations, is a monstrous exotic*

In "Rich Man's War, Rich Man's Fight: Class, Ideology, and Discipline in the Union Army" (*Civil War History* 51 [2005], 269–287), Lorien Foote notes that as more and more volunteers joined the Union army, the class divisions of civil society increasingly became a feature of military society as well. The upper classes, who had the power and prestige to serve as military officers, brought with them particular assumptions about leadership that included hierarchical values and strict discipline based on organizational divisions. The democratic volunteer army of the North, Foote notes, "resented military hierarchy, did not respond well to officers who violated their sense of social equality, and resisted coercion or the enforcement of petty regulations" (270). Whitman here echoes some of the same resistance to military hierarchy on democratic

grounds and believes that the U.S. military needed
somehow to democratize itself, though how that would
occur (soldiers voting whether or not to go into battle?)
remains unspecified, but Whitman was not alone in his
disgust over how officers could treat the "common man"
soldier as an expendable commodity.

[fn] *Pope's council of Cardinals*

The Council of Cardinals, sometimes colloquially
referred to as the "Princes of the Church," is a special
elite group in the Catholic Church, composed of bishops
and archbishops who have been invited to assist the
Pope in Church governance. It is this kind of traditional
hierarchical structure that Whitman finds antithetical to
the development of democracy.

Page 34

*Thus we presume to write, as it were, upon things that exist
not, and travel by maps yet unmade, and a blank*

Alan Trachtenberg, in "Whitman's Visionary Politics,"
comments that "all the difficult complexity and challenge
of Whitman's radical bequest of a democratic politics
inseparable from a democratic poetry lies compacted,
half-hidden" in this passage: "Speech as real as light,
speech as the instrument of vision and vista: such written
speech, like an unmade map of a new, still blank terrain,
was Whitman's most strenuous and challenging notion of
the political" (107).

afflatus

According to the 1876 Webster's, afflatus is (1) a breath or
blast of wind; (2) communication of divine knowledge,
or the power of prophecy; (3) the inspiration of a poet.
Whitman's usage combines these three connotations,
suggesting the strong creative impulse he feels all around
him in the tumult of the present as he seeks to write of
America's future.

splendid eclat of the Democratic principle

> "Éclat" is a French word, meaning (in the 1876 Webster's)
> brilliance or splendor or explosiveness. Here Whitman
> uses the word (in its unaccented American form) to
> indicate the inevitability of the eventual historical
> triumph of the Democratic principle as it bursts forth
> in country after country. Whitman loved using French
> terms that he may well have picked up during his time
> in New Orleans in the 1840s. French terms appear
> frequently in his poetry (as when he originally named his
> "Children of Adam" poems "L'Enfans d'Adam"). There
> are a number of French terms in *Democratic Vistas*, and,
> as the notes at the end of Whitman's essay indicate, he
> was keenly aware of the struggles in France throughout
> the nineteenth century to rid itself of the monarchy and
> institute a democratic republic. His use of French terms
> often indicates his solidarity with those revolutionary
> French efforts, and by using "eclat" to lend a brilliance to
> "the Democratic principle," Whitman suggests that the
> principle is expanding to Europe.

Page 35

Aurora-like

> Aurora is the Roman goddess of dawn, often depicted as
> rising out of the ocean in a chariot.

Page 36

[fn] *great poets and Literatuses*

> Whitman's list of exemplary men and women taken from
> a range of traditions forms a kind of literary history of
> model types, beginning, as Whitman notes, with "primal
> Asia," then into ancient Greece, medieval Europe, and
> finally modern and contemporary Europe: Rama, Arjuna
> are from the Indian Vedas; Solomon from the Christian
> Bible; Achilles, Ulysses, Theseus, Prometheus, Hercules,

Aeneas from ancient Greek mythology; Plutarch's heroes
from Plutarch's biographies of ancient Greeks and
Romans; the Merlin of Celtic bards, the Cid, Arthur and
his knights from legends of medieval knights; Siegfried
and Hagen in the Niebelungen from German and Norse
mythology; Roland and Oliver from *The Song of Roland*
(mid-twelfth century), the oldest surviving major work
of French literature; Roustam in the Shah-Nemah from
Persian epic poetry dating to around AD 1000; Milton's
Satan from *Paradise Lost* by the seventeenth-century
English poet John Milton; Cervantes' Don Quixote from
the Golden Age (sixteenth and seventeenth centuries) in
Spanish literature; Shakespeare's Hamlet, Richard II,
Lear, Marc Antony, &c. from English Renaissance
drama; the modern Faust refers to the character taken
from German folklore but popularized in Christopher
Marlowe's 1604 drama *The Tragical History of Doctor
Faustus* and immortalized in Johann Wolfgang von
Goethe's tragic play *Faust* (1832). Among the women
Whitman mentions here, the Holy Mother is from the
Christian Bible; Cleopatra from ancient Egyptian history;
Penelope from ancient Greek and Roman mythology;
Brunhelde and Chriemhilde in the Niebelungen from
German and Norse mythology; Oriana, Una, &c. from
Celtic mythology; the modern Consuelo from the novel
Consuelo (1842) by the French author George Sand
(a favorite of Whitman's); Walter Scott's Jeanie and Effie
Deans, &c. from Scottish writer Sir Walter Scott's 1818
novel *The Heart of Midlothian*.

Page 40

Idiocrasy of Universalism; Personalism

In theology, universalism is the doctrine of universal
salvation (that all humans will be saved). In *The Pragmatic Whitman: Reimagining American Democracy*,

Stephen John Mack writes that "[t]he phrase 'idiocrasy of universalism' is especially interesting because it captures the paradoxical relationship entailed in the doctrine between the self imagined as autonomous and the ubiquitous culture upon which it depends. Whitman's 'Personalism' is a system of government whereby the individual self rules over itself, but this 'idiocrasy' is only secured and sustained to the extent that it is ideologically informed by a universalized culture. Personalism, then, regards neither the individual nor the collective as supreme to the other in any sense, for they do not jockey for hierarchical position; they are different aspects of the same 'social self,' distinguished only, perhaps, by their respective functions" (145). "Personalism," then, was Whitman's term for radical individualism, but as he makes clear in this essay, such individualism is only one aspect of a self that also owes a debt to universal society, so any "personal" self or identity is always in balance with and contingent upon the larger social constructs in which that self exists: every self is at once idiosyncratic and universal.

Page 45
Long Island

Whitman was born in West Hills, Long Island, and taught school in several Long Island towns as a young man. During Whitman's lifetime, Long Island was known for agriculture, fishing, and shipbuilding. He loved recalling, as he does here, his mother's Long Island memories: see, for example, his poem "The Sleepers," where he tells his mother's story of meeting a young Indian woman.

Page 46
Ophelias

Ophelia is a central character in Shakespeare's *Hamlet*

who tragically lapses into madness and, finally, death. She is portrayed as a sweet and innocent girl who relies on the men in her life to show her how to behave. She has been criticized as one of Shakespeare's most one-dimensional characters.

Enids

Enid is a character from the legends of King Arthur and the Knights of the Round Table. She falls in love with and marries the heroic knight Geraint but then blames herself when he begins to prefer his marriage to his knightly duties. The story of Enid was included in the first set of narrative poems to be published (in 1859) as part of Alfred, Lord Tennyson's *Idylls of the King*.

The day is coming when the deep
questions of woman's entrance

The first conference to address women's rights in the United States was the Seneca Falls Convention of 1848, organized by Elizabeth Cady Stanton and Lucretia Mott, activists in the abolition movement. Stanton and Mott applied the model of human freedom developed by the antislavery movement to women's rights. The Seneca Falls Convention's Declaration of Sentiments, modeled on the Declaration of Independence, called for respect for women as human beings who deserved the same rights as all people and set the agenda for the women's rights movement. At the same time that Whitman was working on *Leaves of Grass*, the press covered the women's rights movement carefully, often publishing full speeches focusing on the definition of American democracy and its inclusion of women, and Whitman read this press coverage. He was also a friend of a number of women's rights activists. While suffrage was the most important issue to the women's rights movement, Whitman focuses in this section of *Democratic Vistas* on work, which was another key concern of the movement. In the period

immediately preceding the publication of *Democratic
Vistas*, Stanton and Susan B. Anthony founded *The
Revolution*, a magazine for women's rights, in 1868, and
in 1869 Stanton and Anthony established the National
Women's Suffrage Association, aimed at passing a
constitutional amendment to grant voting rights to
women. In 1869 Wyoming became the first state to grant
women's suffrage. Whitman supported the movement,
and his work was in turn embraced by many of the early
women's rights activists.

Page 50

under shelter of a delusive and sneaking law

Whitman supported the institution of an international
copyright law, which was hotly debated throughout
the nineteenth century but not enacted until 1891. The
"sneaking law" that was operating when Whitman wrote
Democratic Vistas gave copyright protection to American
authors for works published in the United States but
allowed foreign authors' work to be republished freely
in the United States, thus creating a situation where
American authors' books were more expensive to produce
than books by foreign authors, making it more profitable
for American publishers to publish non-American
writers. As Martin Buinicki in *Negotiating Copyright*
(New York: Routledge, 2006) explains, "while it is the
entire United States 'uttering and absorbing' texts, only
the publishers 'fatten quicker and deeper.' Whitman's
language suggests not theft so much as deception: the
lack of an international copyright law is 'delusive and
sneaking.' . . . [U]nauthorized reprinting represents the
antithesis of democracy, denying honest connection and
open competition. Publishers here are not producers . . .
but rather foragers, refusing to pay fairly for their spoils."

Buinicki shows how Whitman's struggle with foreign
writers is very much wrapped up in his concerns over
international copyright: "he fluctuates between his desire
to praise those European writers who had so greatly
influenced American writers and markets and his desire
to decry them" (116).

Page 51

Old and New Testament

The two parts of the Christian Bible.

Homer

Greek poet, author of the epic poems the *Iliad* and the
Odyssey, dating roughly to the late eighth and early
seventh centuries BC.

Eschylus

Ancient Greek playwright Aeschylus (525–426 BC) is
credited with inventing drama. Only seven of his dozens
of tragedies survive today, including *Seven against Thebes*,
The Suppliants, and the *Oresteia* trilogy.

Plato

Greek philosopher (429–347 BC) who developed the
foundations of Western philosophy.

Juvenal

Roman poet (ca. first–second centuries AD) who wrote
mainly verse satire.

Page 52

codex

In the 1876 Webster's, a codex is a manuscript, a book, or
a code. Whitman here means a printed and bound book, a
form he traces back to the Romans.

Dante

Dante Alighieri (ca. 1265–1321) was a medieval Italian
poet and author of *The Divine Comedy*.

Angelo

Michelangelo Buonarroti (1475–1564) was an Italian
Renaissance painter and sculptor, whose most famous
works include the sculpture *David* and the frescoes
painted on the ceiling of Rome's Sistine Chapel.

Unknown Egyptians . . . Hegel

On display here is Whitman's tendency to borrow
inspiration equally from diverse cultures and traditions.
Encompassed in this web of references are writing and
books; poetry, music, and art; peace, protest, war, and
critique; and politics and philosophy. Of particular
interest in this list are Kant and Hegel [Emmanuel
Kant (1724–1804) and Georg Wilhelm Friedrich Hegel
(1770–1831)], whose philosophy of idealism Whitman was
reading at the time he was writing *Democratic Vistas*.

Page 53

the Amadises and Palmerins of the
13th, 14th, and 15th centuries

The Amadises and Palmerins were the two most popular
series in the popular European books of chivalry, celebrating the deeds of knights (and parodied in Miguel de
Cervantes's *Don Quixote de la Mancha*). The stories are
known for their archetypal characters, episodic structure,
and idealized narratives of adventure and romance.

Page 56

Declaration of Independence . . . the Federal Constitution

To the South, the Declaration of Independence had
become a justification for secession from a tyrannical
federal power, represented in the Constitution. To
slaves and former slaves, the Declaration was read
as a justification for overthrowing their masters. For
Whitman, however, the Declaration put forth the principles of equality and self-determination so important

to his vision of democracy. As Whitman indicates here,
the Constitution at this time was undergoing massive
amendment, as radical Republicans tried to make the
nation's founding document more consonant with the
basic rights of equality espoused by the Declaration.
The Thirteenth Amendment to the Constitution, which
abolished slavery in the United States, was ratified
on December 18, 1865—the First Amendment to the
Federal Constitution in more than sixty years. It was
rather quickly followed by two more "Reconstruction"
amendments: the Fourteenth Amendment (July 9,
1868), giving full citizenship rights to all native-born and
naturalized Americans, including former slaves; and the
Fifteenth Amendment (February 3, 1870), which granted
voting rights to African American men by prohibiting
voting discrimination based on "race, color, or previous
condition of servitude."

Page 59
stump-speech

> An electioneering speech, often made from atop a tree
> stump or some other elevated platform.

Page 60
Four Years' War

> The American Civil War, which lasted from 1861 to 1865.
> Whitman often spoke of the importance of the war to
> his poetic practice as well as to the formation of the
> American character, and here he underscores those claims
> once again. The Civil War was known at the time by many
> different names, including the War to Preserve the Union,
> the War of Secession, and (the term most favored in the
> South) the War Between the States; in England, the Civil
> War was commonly known as The American War.

Long ere the Second Centennial arrives

When Whitman first reprinted *Democratic Vistas* in
his 1876 book, *Two Rivulets*, he used the unaltered
electrotype plates of the original 1871 edition of the
essay. He initially printed only a hundred copies of *Two
Rivulets* and then, a few months later, reprinted the book,
this time in a run of eight hundred copies. During these
months between printings, he clearly re-read *Democratic
Vistas* and found several typographical errors, which
he corrected by having alterations made in the plates.
While he was re-reading the essay, he also noted an
embarrassing sentence, speaking of "the hundredth year
of this Union" as an event that had not yet occurred. Since
Two Rivulets was part of Whitman's "Centennial Edition"
of his works, prepared to celebrate the centennial of the
United States in 1876, this statement obviously dated
his essay. In addition, his original prophecy that there
would be, on America's hundredth birthday, "some forty
to fifty great States, among them Canada and Cuba"
obviously had not been fulfilled, so Whitman carefully
substituted a phrase of the exact length (as was necessary
when altering plates): "Long ere the Second Centennial
arrives" replaced "When the hundredth year of this Union
arrives." Whitman thus kept the prophecy but gave it
another century to come true. By July 4, 1876, there were
thirty-seven states in the Union; Colorado was admitted
in August of that year, making thirty-eight. By the second
centennial, there were indeed fifty states, though, of
course Canada and Cuba were not among them. (This
whole paragraph continued to vex Whitman, since, by
extending the prophecy for a century, he seemed to be
suggesting that the population of the country would
reach "sixty or seventy millions" only by 1976. But the U.S.
population was already nearly forty million by 1870—an
increase of well over 20 percent in ten years despite the

loss of nearly a million lives in the Civil War—and by
1880 was over fifty million, so when Whitman reprinted
Democratic Vistas in *Specimen Days and Collect* (1882),
he modified the sentence about population to indicate
that it would reach "sixty or seventy millions" by the
time "the present century closes." In fact, the population
by 1890 was already well over sixty million and by 1900
exceeded seventy-six million.)

Page 61
Puritans

The Puritans were a Christian group that broke from
the Church of England and founded Plymouth Colony
in New England in 1620. They rejected the "worldliness"
of society and based their beliefs on Calvinism with its
insistence on the total depravity of humankind.

[fn] *general prevalence of that fervid comradeship*

Whitman here continues to move the relationships he
explored in his "Calamus" poems—bonds of affection
between males—from the personal to the political.
The "Calamus" poems are often read as one of the
first articulations of what came to be gay identity, but
Whitman always argued that they were finally a vision
of a society transformed by a new intensity of affection
that transcended conventional romantic love. Gay Wilson
Allen in the *Walt Whitman Handbook* suggested that
"here Whitman's Calamus sentiments become completely
socialized and emotionally reinforce his democratic
idealism" (191).

[fn] *adhesive*

Whitman borrowed this term from phrenology, the study
of the relationship between a person's character and
the shape of his or her skull. As a way of articulating an
emerging sense of affectional relationships necessary in a
democracy, adhesiveness suggested attachment between

people (or groups of people), including friendship, brotherhood, and love, sometimes physical. Such attachment was, Whitman felt, the only way true equality could exist, and equality was for Whitman a necessary element of democracy. Whitman also sometimes used the term "amativeness" to indicate love between men and women that was usually sexual (as in the "Children of Adam" cluster). Adhesiveness, then, carries a broader connotation than amativeness, is more commonly associated with friendship, and is for Whitman associated with democracy; Whitman develops this phrenological term into a term that covers intense male-male affectional bonds.

Page 64
Idealism

In the philosophy of perception, Idealism is the notion that the world is inseparable from our mind's perception of it, in contrast to Realism, or the idea that the world exists independently from its perceiver. Here Whitman champions Idealism's embrace of experience that cannot be explained rationally as an antidote to "the growing excess and arrogance of realism."

Page 65
[fn] *The Indian Vedas, the Nackas of Zoroaster, The Talmud of the Jews, the Old Testament also, the Gospel of Christ and his disciples, Plato's works, the Koran of Mohammed, the Edda of Snorro, and so on toward our own day, to Swedenborg*

As suggested in this passage, Whitman finds—in the joining of religion and poetry that represents the highest form of literature—a literature that can guide American democracy. Once again on display here is the way in which Whitman borrows inspiration equally from diverse cultures and traditions—Hinduism (the Indian Vedas),

the ancient Persian religion of Zoroastrianism (the
Nackas), Judaism (the Talmud and the Old Testament),
Christianity (the Old Testament and the Gospel), Classical
Greek philosophy (Plato's works), Islam (the Koran),
medieval Norse mythology (the Edda), and eighteenth-
century Christian mysticism (Swedenborg).

Leibnitz, Kant and Hegel

Gottfried Wilhelm von Leibnitz (var: Leibniz) (1646–
1716), Emmanuel Kant (1724–1804), and Georg Wilhelm
Friedrich Hegel (1770–1831) were German philosophers
who, in different ways, sought an integration of the mind
and nature. Leibnitz's philosophy of Rationalism, for
example, attempted to reconcile religion and science and
to find harmony between the senses and understanding.
In *Critique of Pure Reason* (1781), Kant argues that some
things (the existence of God, the fate of the human soul)
are beyond reason (and Kant asserts that his "might
well be the true apology for Leibniz, even against those
of his disciples who heap praises upon him that do him
no honor" [2002: 336]). Hegel's notion of dialectical
reasoning argues that the contemplation of an idea and
its opposite can result in a synthesis of the two that
represents a higher level of thought. At the time that
Whitman wrote *Democratic Vistas* he was engrossed
in the reading of German philosophy; in *Whitman the
Political Poet*, Betsy Erkkila writes: "In his attempt to
reconcile the ideals of democracy with the carnage of
war and the corruptions of post-Civil War America,
Whitman found philosophical support in the ideas of
Hegel and the German idealistic thinkers. . . . Hegel's
idea of a triplicate process through which opposites are
merged in a higher synthesis, and his vision of history
as a manifestation of spirit rationalized Whitman's own
vision of American democracy progressing through the
evils and contradictions of the present toward divine

ends" (248). Even the structure of *Democratic Vistas*
itself, Erkkila notes, is Hegelian in its working through
of contradictions.

Page 67
the Librarian of Congress

Ainsworth Rand Spofford, Librarian from 1864–1897.
Spofford's name appears on the copyright page of the
final "death-bed" edition of *Leaves of Grass*, confirming
Whitman's claims of copyright.

Page 68
great poems of Death

Here Whitman calls for the new American poets to
compose "great poems of Death," because in his mind
democracy required that death be viewed in terms
"consistent with modern science" and seen as a natural
part of the endless flux and change of the Kosmos;
democratic poets would then finally remove death from
the grip of religions, which used superstitions about death
and afterlife and heaven and hell to institute hierarchy
and to control human behavior. A democratic conception
of death would break down this hierarchy and undermine
artificial categories like "good" and "evil."

Page 69
Lucretius

Titus Lucretius Carus (ca. 99 BC–ca. 55 BC) was a Roman
poet and philosopher and author of the epic poem *De
rerum natura* (*On the Nature of the Universe*), an account
of the world through atomic physics. Whitman is offering
Lucretius's joining of poetry and science as a model for
contemporary poets of America; America, Whitman
argues, needs poets who "confront Time and Space"

"both with science and *con amore* [with love]," who see
(as Whitman said in "Song of Myself") that "every atom
belonging to me as good belongs to you."

Page 70

who shall hold in behemoth? who bridle leviathan?

Behemoth and Leviathan are Biblical creatures (of land
and sea, respectively) thought to be unconquerable
because of their enormous size and power. Like the
behemoth that cannot be held in or the leviathan that
cannot be bridled, America's future is, to Whitman
here, an enormous and uncontrollable uncertainty that
nevertheless must be grappled with. Betsy Erkkila in
Whitman the Political Poet sees this question of who
shall bridle leviathan as "the very center" of *Democratic
Vistas*: "It is to literature, and to the poet in particular,
that Whitman looked for the power that would bridle
the gilded monsters to which America, and perhaps
the theory of America, had given birth." Behemoth and
Leviathan, in this reading, are the "new lords of capital"
who control America's wealth (250–251). The image of
the leviathan as the social state echoes back, of course, to
Thomas Hobbes's *Leviathan* (1651).

Short as the span of our national life has been

Whitman sometimes liked to date his works by an American calendar, counting the years from the beginning of
the United States, which he marked as the reading of
the Declaration of Independence in 1776. Thus on the
title page of his 1860–61 edition of *Leaves of Grass*, the
date is given as "Year 85 of The States." At the time of
the publication of *Democratic Vistas*, the country was
fast approaching its first centennial, and Whitman would
reprint his essay in his *Two Rivulets* volume, issued for
the country's centennial in 1876.

Page 71

[fn] *The Labor Question*

This footnote was deleted when Whitman republished
Democratic Vistas in *Specimen Days and Collect* (1882).
As Betsy Erkkila in *Whitman the Political Poet* notes,
Whitman here "returned to the anticapitalist rhetoric
of his early years": "It is in the growing conflict between
labor and capital, rich and poor, that he sees the most
dangerous current of the future" (250). As that division
grew in the Gilded Age, it is revealing that Whitman
excised this powerful passage, as he became less and less
comfortable confronting the economic conditions that
were undermining the ideal of democratic equality.

[fn] *Asiatic immigration on our Pacific side*

Large-scale immigration of Asians, particularly Chinese,
to the United States started in the mid-1800s in response
to the California Gold Rush. By 1851 there were twenty-
five thousand Chinese living and working in California.
Many native-born Americans resented the fact that the
Chinese were willing to work for less than most non-
Asian workers, and this resentment eventually escalated
into violence that went on for decades. In an attempt
to limit Chinese immigration, Congress passed a law
forbidding American vessels from transporting Chinese
immigrants to the United States. This was followed by
the Naturalization Act of 1870, passed while Whitman
was preparing *Democratic Vistas* for publication; this
act restricted U.S. naturalization to "white persons and
persons of African descent," making all others ineligible
for citizenship. In 1882 the Chinese Exclusion Act would
restrict Chinese immigration specifically.

[fn] *squads of vagabond children*

Street-wandering children were a significant social
problem in the 1860s and 1870s. One *New York Times*

article reports that roughly twelve thousand children each year sought the assistance of New York City shelter houses aimed specifically at the care of destitute children ("Street Waifs," *New York Times*, July 20, 1869, 2).

[fn] *hideousness and squalor of certain quarters of the cities*
The Five Points district of New York was one of the worst of these "certain quarters," described by one reporter as "the very sink of abject poverty and moral pollution, worse by far than any heathen country to which missionaries are sent at such great expense." Significantly, the reporter notes that such destitution did not necessarily make it the most dangerous district, with worse violence to be found "on Houston Street, or even Broadway" ("Life in the Slums," *New York Times*, August 21, 1870, 8).

[fn] *pompous, nauseous, outside shows of vulgar wealth*
The gap between rich and poor began to quickly widen after the Civil War with America's growing capitalistic system, leading to the United States having the largest wealth disparity of all industrialized nations. At the time he wrote *Democratic Vistas*, Whitman was experiencing the early manifestations of a "conspicuous consumption" culture.

[fn] *new Juvenal*
See the note on Juvenal on page 51.

[fn] *our system of inflated paper-money currency*
In order to finance the Civil War, the U.S. government passed the Legal Tender Act in 1862, which authorized the creation of "greenbacks," or paper money that could not be redeemed for silver or gold. When the value of this paper currency decreased, it became the subject of heated controversy.

[fn] *theory and practice of a protective tariff*
See the note on tariff on page 5.

Page 74

To furnish, therefore, something like escape

Whitman omitted this paragraph when he republished *Democratic Vistas* in *Specimen Days and Collect*. It is a powerful passage in which Whitman defines his new "class" of "Literatuses" and, as he often does in *Democratic Vistas*, strains his sight to make out just what this future group of democratic artists would be like. Ironically, he falls back on comparing them to the "Judean prophets" of the past "with their flashes of power, wisdom, and poetic beauty, lawless as lightning." But they are still "indefinite," as is so much of what Whitman discerns as he strains to make out shapes in his democratic vistas.

we now proceed to note, as on the hopeful terraces or platforms of our history

When Whitman republished *Democratic Vistas* in *Specimen Days and Collect* (1882), he omitted the rest of this paragraph, beginning with "we now proceed to note," along with the following three paragraphs, which prophesy what will emerge in "a few years," including a vital American opera, complete with acoustically sound concert halls in which a new native music will be heard; a renewed tradition of American oratory, with previously unimagined power and wisdom; and vast new museums with wise guides who will teach the nation's youth all they should know of natural human history. By 1882, Whitman was more cautious about predicting America's immediate future, excising the prophecies that already had not come true and emphasizing instead a more distant future of fulfillment.

Page 78

in ceaseless succession through Time

When Whitman republished *Democratic Vistas* in *Specimen Days and Collect* (1882), he added the following phrase to this sentence: "—the main thing being the average, the bodily, the concrete, the democratic, the popular, on which all the superstructures of the future are to permanently rest." He then deleted the final paragraph and ended the essay with that phrase. The final paragraph of the 1871 *Specimen Days* is therefore not generally known; it is remarkable for its expression of fear for the American present mixed with hope for its future.

General Notes section

When Whitman republished *Democratic Vistas* in *Specimen Days and Collect* (1882), he deleted the General Notes. He reprinted parts of these notes elsewhere in *Specimen Days and Collect*, but some parts of these notes were never again reprinted. They add an immediacy to Whitman's essay by bringing events right up to the time of publication in 1871.

Page 79
"Society"

Whitman was critical of socialites (or "Society" or the "haut-ton coteries" as he called them on page 19) in particular because he felt their materialism and selfishness was a detriment to democracy as he envisioned it.

Washington City

Washington, D.C.

high life below stairs business

John Collet's 1763 painting *High Life Below Stairs* is a satirical depiction of servants imitating their masters' aristocratic behavior and fashionable attire. Similarly, Whitman is laughing at how the mechanics and farmers of America play at being "fashionable" instead of celebrating their own rough-hewn beauty.

illy-played

> played badly

man and woman, (far, far greater words
than "gentleman" and "lady,")

> Whitman argued for getting rid of words like "gentleman"
> and "lady" that derived from feudalistic and aristocratic
> traditions, and he was frustrated to see such terms
> adopted in American usage because they embodied
> expectations of a certain kind of class-inflected behavior.
> In *Specimen Days*, he noted when he saw "the women
> of the West" that "I am not so well satisfied with what I
> see of the women of the prairie cities. . . . The ladies . . .
> are all fashionably drest, and have the look of 'gentility'
> in face, manner and action, but they do *not* have, either
> in physique or the mentality appropriate to them, any
> high native originality of spirit or body. . . . They are
> 'intellectual' and fashionable, but dyspeptic-looking
> and generally doll-like; their ambition evidently is to
> copy their eastern sisters. Something far different and
> in advance must appear. . . ."

Page 80

Victor Hugo

> Hugo (1802–1885), the French writer and human rights
> advocate, was the author of *Les Misérables* (1862), one of
> the great novels of social injustice. A passionate supporter
> of the French Republic, he became a fierce antagonist
> of Napoleon III, who was deposed just as Whitman was
> finishing *Democratic Vistas*; the restoration of the French
> Republic allowed Hugo to return to Paris after nearly two
> decades in exile. While Whitman had reservations about
> Hugo's writing, he always admired Hugo's commitment
> to justice, and he liked to quote Hugo's "L'Année Terrible,"
> his long poetic meditation about the 1870–1871 year,
> when France was defeated in the Prussian War and

Napoleon III was deposed. "A whole world," as Whitman
paraphrases Hugo, "if it is wrong, does not outweigh one
just man" (*DBN* 656; *NUPM* 1856).

Byron

George Gordon, Lord Byron (1788–1824), one of the
best-known and most accomplished British Romantic
poets, was known for his lifelong battles against tyranny
and injustice, but he became even better known for his
sensational love life, including relationships with young
men, very young women, a married woman, and his half-
sister. He traveled widely in search of romance and in the
service of revolutionary change, supporting Greek fighters
seeking independence from the Ottoman Empire. He was
preparing to lead a rebel force in an attack on a Turkish
fortress when he fell ill and died. His body was returned
to England, but according to a number of accounts, his
heart was removed and buried in Greece.

Pharos

An ancient Egyptian lighthouse, considered one of the
seven wonders of the ancient world, dating to the third
century BC, built on the island of Pharos (in Alexandria)
from which it took its name. Ships were said to be able to
detect its light at night or its smoke during the day up to
one hundred miles away.

Page 81

the great poems of Asian antiquity

Whitman repeats here what he said in the main body of
the essay. For these specific works, see the previous notes.

Page 82

Greek dramatists

Greek dramatists, most notably Aeschylus, Euripides,
and Sophocles, are credited with the creation of poetic
tragedy.

Hamlet

> This early modern tragedy written by Shakespeare and first performed c. 1602 ends with the deaths of the entire royal family.

Walter Scott

> Sir Walter Scott (1771–1832) was a popular Scottish novelist and poet whose works include *Ivanhoe* and *Rob Roy*. Whitman was fond of, and was influenced by, Scott's ballads. He returned to Scott again and again throughout his life, and once noted "How much I am indebted to Scott. . . . I couldn't tell it myself" (*WWWC* 1:96). Nonetheless, he never reprinted this parenthetical celebration of Scott as Shakespeare's equal.

THE LATE WAR

> Whitman never reprinted the first paragraph of this note—one of his most powerful condemnations of the "Slave-Holding power"—after he omitted it in *Specimen Days and Collect* (1882).

The Secession War

> The U.S. Civil War was sometimes known as the Secession War because it was precipitated in part by eleven southern U.S. states declaring their secession from the United States and forming the Confederate States of America.

abolition of Slavery . . . extirpation of the Slaveholding Class

> Slavery was abolished in the United States in 1865 via constitutional amendment (the Thirteenth Amendment).

Radical Democracy

> Whitman's assertion of individual rights within the national collectivity is a form of Radical Democracy, which is the notion that democracy depends on difference and dissent.

the removal of serfdom in Russia, slavery in the United States, and of the meanest of Imperialisms in France

> In Imperial Russia, 80 percent of the population were

peasants, many of whom lived in serfdom. While
they, unlike American slaves, were not considered the
property of landowners, they were not allowed to leave
the property on which they were born, and they were
forced to make regular payments to the landowner in
labor and goods. The Emancipation Reform of 1861
ended the serfdom of most Russian peasants; those on
imperial properties and private estates were freed by the
Emancipation Manifesto of 1866. Slavery officially ended
in the United States with the passing of the Thirteenth
Amendment to the Constitution in 1865. Whitman's
reference to the "Imperialisms in France" is more
slippery. The French colonies used slaves as manpower
for sugarcane plantations in the 1700s, and the Haitian
Revolution in the 1790s was a successful slave uprising
against French colonial power. France abolished slavery
(for the second time) in 1848. France, too, of course, had
undergone the French Revolution from 1789 to 1799,
overthrowing the French monarchy and its feudalistic
ways and paving the way for a government based on
citizens' rights. The nineteenth-century history of France,
however, was a dizzying ride, as hopes for a new republic
were followed by the restoration of the monarchy, a
reformed and limited monarchy, another revolution in
1848, a second republic, and a second and growingly
authoritarian empire under Napoleon III, which came
to an end in the Franco-Prussian War just as Whitman
was finishing *Democratic Vistas* in 1870. Napoleon III's
demise opened the way for a third French republic and an
end, in Whitman's mind, of France's "mean Imperialisms."
The short-lived Paris Commune, a workers' uprising and
takeover of Paris in the spring of 1871, was to occur just
after *Democratic Vistas* was published. See Whitman's
final note on page 84.

Page 83

seeds of the Crusades

> The Crusades were a series of military campaigns in the
> Middle Ages carried out by European Christians against
> Muslims in the Middle East. The eight Crusades (plus
> what later became known as the Children's Crusade)
> spanned some two hundred years and their effects on
> Western civilization are far-reaching. Not only did they
> lead to the decline of feudalism, since thousands of
> wealthy landowners sold or mortgaged their property to
> raise money for crusades, but they also led to a surge in
> cultural development due to the broadened experiences
> and tastes occasioned by contact with unfamiliar people
> and places.

GENERAL SUFFRAGE, ELECTIONS

> See the discussion in the introduction of Whitman's
> attitudes toward the expansion of voting rights, especially
> the Fifteenth Amendment to the Constitution (which
> guaranteed voting rights to male former slaves). Whit-
> man's disdain for politicians was long-standing, and
> some of his earlier writings, like "The Eighteenth Presi-
> dency," are vitriolic in their disgust with elected American
> leaders.

pecuniary interest of rings

> "Rings" is a then-recent slang term for organizations that
> tried to control politics or local affairs in their own interest.

STATE RIGHTS

> Whitman never reprinted this note after he omitted it in
> *Specimen Days and Collect* (1882). He is here trying to
> articulate one of the great paradoxes of U.S. identity—
> one nation made up of separate states. Whitman always
> tried to walk the tightrope between federalism and states'
> rights, but in order to preserve the Union, he had to "favor
> generalization, consolidation."

imperial Union

Whitman's notion of an "imperial Union" acknowledges the paradox inherent in his concept of a democratic America: the need for individuals, guided by independent thinking, to willingly submit to the national collectivity. This is one of Whitman's strongest affirmations of his federalist leaning: individual and state rights must yield finally to Nationality.

Page 84

LATEST FROM EUROPE

Whitman never reprinted this note after he omitted it in *Specimen Days and Collect* (1882). Its reporting of late-breaking events in Europe adds an immediacy to the original publication of *Democratic Vistas* and extends Whitman's U.S.-centered view of democracy to a more international perspective.

Franco-German war-news (as of Sept. 19, 1870)

The Franco-German (or Franco-Prussian) War took place July 19, 1870, to May 10, 1871. A coalition of German states, led by Prussia, defeated France. The defeat marked the end of French hegemony in continental Europe and resulted in the creation of a unified Germany.

Louis Napoleon

Louis Napoleon (1808–1873), also known as Napo-leon III, was French leader from 1848–1870. He was elected president of the Second French Republic in 1848, and then, since the new constitution mandated only a single term for a president and he could not convince the National Assembly to alter it, he staged a coup d'etat in 1851 and set up the Second French Empire. During the 1860s, there was a series of popular uprisings against Napoleon III's empire, and France continued to struggle toward a republican form of government. Napoleon III

was captured at the Battle of Sedan (in the Franco-
German War) on September 2, 1870, and deposed
two days later. Whitman makes clear his disdain for
Napoleon III with his reference to the emperor's "rat-
cunning" ways.

Republican forms

The third French republic was set up after the demise of
Napoleon III in 1870, and Whitman, always a supporter
of the French revolution and France's attempts to become
a republic, ends *Democratic Vistas* with an up-to-the
moment call for America's "affinity" with the "cause
of Popular Government" in Europe, "and especially in
France." The momentous events taking place in France
allowed Whitman, in these appended notes, to extend
his democratic vistas beyond the borders of the United
States.

King of Prussia

King Wilhelm I (1797–1888), also known as Wilhelm
the Great, was King of Prussia from 1861 to 1888 and
the first German emperor from 1871 to 1888. Under
his leadership Germany won the Franco-German war.
Whitman concludes *Democratic Vistas* by mocking "his
majesty," the Prussian "King," for choosing the wrong side
of history in "refus[ing] to treat, on any terms, with a
government risen out of Democracy." Such governments,
Whitman believed, would inevitably rise throughout
Europe and eventually throughout the world; they were
the democratic vistas he saw on history's horizon.

{ Selected Bibliography }
of Works about *Democratic Vistas*

For many decades after Whitman's death, *Democratic Vistas* received little extended commentary. The American poet Hart Crane, writing to the poet and critic Allen Tate in 1930 about Crane's book-length poem *The Bridge*, which responded in striking ways to Whitman, complained to Tate that "you, like so many others, never seem to have read his *Democratic Vistas* and other of his statements sharply decrying the materialism, industrialism, etc., of which you name him the guilty and hysterical spokesman." Crane here captures both the disregard into which Whitman's essay had sunk, and the paradox that lies at the heart of the essay: Whitman, the perceived celebrator and singer of America, could also be the nation's most severe critic.

It was not until fifteen years after Crane's comment that critics began to seriously reconsider *Democratic Vistas*. Lionel Trilling and Malcolm Cowley, in brief notes in the mid-1940s, began to suggest that Whitman's essay deserved reconsideration, and Edward F. Grier offered the first extended study of the history of the composition and publication of *Democratic Vistas* in 1951. But not until Richard V. Chase's 1955 *Walt Whitman Reconsidered* did the essay receive an extended reading. Chase's chapter on "The Theory of America" offered an interpretation of the essay that opened the door to increasingly sophisticated and innovative approaches to Whitman's text. The following bibliography traces, in chronological order, some of the most important critical arguments with *Democratic Vistas* over the past sixty-five years. A more extensive list of criticism is Donald D. Kummings, "The Prose Writings: Selected Secondary Sources," in Donald D. Kummings, ed., *A Companion to Walt Whitman* (Malden, Massachusetts: Blackwell, 2006), 576–579.

Trilling, Lionel. "Sermon on a Text from Whitman." *Nation* 160 (February 24, 1945), 215–220. Explores Whitman's theory of "Personalism" in *Democratic Vistas* and argues that Whitman is as much a poet of the individual as of the masses.

Allen, Gay Wilson. "*Democratic Vistas*, 1871." In *Walt Whitman Handbook* (Chicago: Packard and Company, 1946), 186–192. Views *Democratic Vistas* as Whitman's first "serious contribution to prose literature" and analyzes his program for a "new democratic literature." Allen revised this short essay for his *New Walt Whitman Handbook* (New York: New York University Press, 1976), 201–205, where he found less to like about *Democratic Vistas*, calling it "wordy, turgid, and syntactically distracting."

Cowley, Malcolm. "Walt Whitman: The Philosopher." *New Republic* 146 (September 29, 1947), 29–31. Argues that Whitman is an unsuccessful philosopher because he has "quarreling tendencies" that interfere with any clear statement of a thesis, but finds *Democratic Vistas* his most successful exercise in consecutive thinking.

Grier, Edward F. "Walt Whitman, the *Galaxy*, and *Democratic Vistas.*" *American Literature* 23 (November 1951), 332–350. Lays out in detail the original serial publication of *Democratic Vistas* in the *Galaxy*, including the decision by the *Galaxy* not to publish the third of Whitman's essays.

Chase, Richard. *Walt Whitman Reconsidered* (New York: William Sloane, 1955). Chapter 5, "The Theory of America" (153–165), calls *Democratic Vistas* "an admirable and characteristic diatribe," perhaps "too simply and schematically reasoned" and lacking "an adequate sense of disorder"; examines the essay as "a transcendental version of Jeffersonian-Jacksonian democracy" that reveals "Whitman's lifelong distrust of government" and his "disillusion with practical politics," wherein "his lifelong belief in free trade is spiritualized into a vision of international amity"; and suggests that "*Democratic Vistas* is a kind of American version of [Matthew] Arnold's *Culture and Anarchy*."

Marx, Leo. "*Democratic Vistas*: Notes for a Discussion." *Emerson Society Quarterly* 22 (1961), 12–15. Offers a number of questions that need to be asked about *Democratic Vistas*, including its relationship to Carlyle's "Shooting Niagara," its structure, its themes, its conception of democratic culture, and Whitman's role as a social prophet.

Reeves, Paschal. "The Silhouette of the State in *Democratic Vistas*—Hegelian or Whitmanian?" *Personalist* 43 (Summer 1962), 374–382. Argues that *Democratic Vistas* reveals that Hegel and Whitman differ radically in their views of the form, function, and motivation of the State, with Hegel an apologist for a totalitarian order and Whitman the militant prophet of a democratic republic.

Blodgett, Harold W. "*Democratic Vistas*—100 Years After." In Karl Schubert and Ursula Müller-Richter, eds., *Geschichte und Gesellschaft in der amerikanischen Literatur* (Heidelberg: Quelle & Meyer, 1975), 114–131. Reviews the publication history and main ideas of *Democratic Vistas*, noting that a century after its publication the essay continues to be neglected, and claims that in fact it is "the most remarkable single pronouncement upon American democracy in American literature."

Scholnick, Robert J. "The American Context of *Democratic Vistas*." In Joann P. Krieg, ed., *Walt Whitman: Here and Now* (Westport, Connecticut: Greenwood, 1985), 147–156. Argues that "the greatness of [*Specimen Days*] is due to its ability to combine a realistic and unsparing evaluation of both the contemporary failings and the structural weaknesses of democracy with a full statement of its spiritual potential," and examines other American writers (like E. L. Godkin, O. B. Frothingham, and especially Eugene Benson) who were "denounc[ing] the corruption" of postbellum American society.

Weisbuch, Robert. *Atlantic Double-Cross: American Litera-ture and British Influence in the Age of Emerson* (Chicago: University of Chicago Press, 1986). Chapter 4, "Whitman's Personalism, Arnold's Culture" (83–106), examines Matthew Arnold as "the rejected muse" of *Democratic Vistas*, exam-ining "the social differences which an American literature proposed and the English model of an ideal society which it refused," and tracing the deep differences between the two writers, with Arnold looking to the past and what "has been" and Whitman looking to the future and "what has never been."

Erkkila, Betsy. *Whitman the Political Poet* (New York: Oxford University Press, 1989). Chapter 10, "Who Bridle Leviathan?" (240–259), offers a cogent reading of *Democratic Vistas* as Whitman's critique of the Gilded Age and the emergent "new lords of capital" who are creating a "growing conflict be-tween labor and capital, rich and poor"; Whitman thus be-comes "one of the first major writers to chart the potentially downward spiral of American history in the postwar years," as he calls for "the repoliticization of the literature of the future," seeking ways "to reconcile the desire for personal lib-erty with the demands of social union," "moving closer to the socialist concept of the individual finding her or his greatest freedom within a political community."

Pascal, Richard. "'Dimes on the Eyes': Walt Whitman and the Pursuit of Wealth in America." *Nineteenth-Century Litera-ture* 44 (September 1989), 141–172. Examines in part of the essay the ways that Whitman in *Democratic Vistas* employs "capitalism's basic vocabulary in order to undermine some of its basic assumptions."

Aspiz, Harold. "The Body Politic in *Democratic Vistas*." In Ed Folsom, ed., *Walt Whitman: The Centennial Essays* (Iowa City: University of Iowa Press, 1994), 105–119. Tracks how in *Democratic Vistas* Whitman appropriated the common-place "body politic trope" and transformed it into a strikingly original physical metaphor, portraying the nation as an organism with bodily functions.

Mancuso, Luke. "'Reconstruction is still in Abeyance': Walt Whitman's *Democratic Vistas* and the Federalizing of National Identity." *American Transcendental Quarterly* 8 (September 1994), 229–250. Offers a careful reading of *Democratic Vistas* in the context of the national debates over the passage of the Fifteenth Amendment to the Constitution, and in the context of the women's suffrage movement, arguing that Whitman sought to be "a mediator between factions," casting "his reconciliation between federalists and states' rights advocates in the future tense," challenging "the divided past to begin to reconstruct its future as a network of collaborative social relations between races and sections," and taking on for himself a unique "federalizing role" to propose a new "'ensemble' identity in the United States"—"a collaborative governmental infrastructure founded on federal and state interdependence in the enactment of 'Radical Democracy.'" This essay appears in a revised form as Chapter 2 of Mancuso's *The Strange Sad War Revolving: Walt Whitman, Reconstruction, and the Emergence of Black Citizenship, 1865–1876* (Columbia, South Carolina: Camden House, 1997), 51–76.

Trachtenberg, Alan. "Whitman's Visionary Politics." In Geoffrey Sill, ed., *Walt Whitman of Mickle Street: A Centennial Collection* (Knoxville: University of Tennessee Press, 1994), 94–108. Focuses on Whitman's "terms for vision, for seeing (the act), sight (the name of the act), and vista (what is seen in the widest, most distant and panoramic sense) in *Democratic Vistas*," and argues that Whitman's task is to make us see that "we must believe in a future different from the present in order to believe in the present," a task requiring "multiple acts of vision," since "visibility is the method and also the theme, the means and end of this extraordinary work," which culminates when "vision completes itself in language."

Warren, James Perrin. "Reconstructing Language in *Democratic Vistas*." In Ed Folsom, ed., *Walt Whitman: The Centennial Essays* (Iowa City: University of Iowa Press, 1994), 79–87. Analyzes Whitman's "reconstructive strategies" in *Democratic Vistas*, noting that reconstruction for Whitman is as much textual as political; demonstrates that *Vistas* has its roots in Whitman's antebellum writing.

Reynolds, David S. *Walt Whitman's America: A Cultural Biography* (New York: Knopf, 1995). Chapter 14, "Reconstructing a Nation, Reconstructing a Poet: Postbellum Institutions" (448–494), contains two sections ("Undemocratic Vistas" and "Taking Care of Business," 463–484) that place *Democratic Vistas* in its cultural contexts, as Whitman "began to view America's social problems as overwhelming, beyond immediate poetic repair"; views the essay as "a patchwork document that changed dramatically over time," embodying Whitman's "conflicting tendencies toward conservatism and radicalism," sending "mixed signals" on "the issue of blacks and slavery" while "siding ideologically" with President Andrew Johnson "in his simultaneous devotion to the Union and to states' rights" and in his attempts to reabsorb the South into the Union without punishing the Confederates; analyzes Whitman's response to Carlyle's "Shooting Niagara" and argues that Whitman does not reject Carlyle but, through his emerging "Hegelian outlook," incorporates "both Carlylean cynicism and Darwinian materialism" into an overall positive assessment of America's future.

Jay, Paul. *Contingency Blues: The Search for Foundations in American Criticism* (Madison: University of Wisconsin Press, 1997). Chapter 2, "Emerson, Whitman, and the Problem of Culture," 42–56, analyzes *Democratic Vistas* in light of Emerson's essays on "aesthetics and culture," arguing that "Whitman's stress on the whole issue of modernization" and "his desire to sketch out a 'programme' for culture in America" mark "a difference in emphasis from Emerson," though both writers "share an idealist commitment to the metaphysical as ground."

Teichgraeber III, Richard F. "'Culture' in Industrializing America." *Intellectual History Newsletter* 21 (1999), 11–23. Seeks to suggest the "largely unwritten history of the concept of culture in the industrial era," beginning with *Democratic Vistas*, seen here as "one of the most powerful statements of an understanding of culture that is democratic and inclusive, rather than hierarchical and elitist"; reads *Vistas* in the context of other writers (James Freeman Clarke, Richard Ely, W. E. B. DuBois) who were writing about "self-culture" in an era when "new cultural institutions" were being created at an unprecedented rate and "the American rhetoric of culture" was developing.

Cmiel, Kenneth. "Whitman the Democrat." In David S. Reynolds, ed., *A Historical Guide to Walt Whitman* (New York: Oxford University Press, 2000), 205–233. Sets out to answer the question, "What were Whitman's politics?," and argues that "Whitman's political ideas became a mesh of his working-class background and literary aspirations" as he blended liberal positions with democratic ones and became "a liberal defender of freedom and a radical democrat," moving from artisanal democracy in the 1840s to "transcendental democracy" in the 1850s and finally, by the 1870s, to a "stale retreat" from "both the individual and democratic sides of his project," finally failing in *Democratic Vistas* to contribute to a necessary rethinking of liberalism or democracy.

Folsom, Ed. "Lucifer and Ethiopia: Whitman, Race, and Poetics before the Civil War and After." In David S. Reynolds, ed., *A Historical Guide to Walt Whitman* (New York: Oxford University Press, 2000), 45–95. Investigates how, "during his career, Whitman's attitudes toward African Americans altered significantly"; focuses on "two key figures in his poetry, the only two black characters to whom he gave voice in *Leaves of Grass*: 'Lucifer,' a young male slave who

appears in Whitman's 1855 poem that he eventually named
'The Sleepers,' and 'Ethiopia,' an old female emancipated
slave who appears in his 1870 poem 'Ethiopia Saluting the
Colors'"; examines how "Ethiopia" relates to *Democratic
Vistas*.

Mack, Stephen John. *The Pragmatic Whitman: Reimagining
American Democracy* (Iowa City: University of Iowa Press,
2002). Demonstrates how pragmatism serves as a useful
"interpretive strategy" to "produce worthwhile readings" of
a number of Whitman's texts, including *Democratic Vistas*;
Chapter 7, "'The Divine Literatus Comes': Religion and
Poetry in the Cultivation of Democratic Selfhood" (135–
159), analyzes how, for Whitman, "prose writing often entailed a special burden of precision," and examines *Vistas*
as Whitman's "most profound and sustained meditation on
democratic life," offering "a comprehensive theory of democratic culture and also an ambitious program, informed by
his own native pragmatism, for the re-mediation of American culture and the full democratization of American society," culminating in "the notion of a secular, democratic
religion" that would require "a deep emotional and spiritual
understanding of the complex material ties that bind people
together in a web of mutual obligation"; *Vistas*, then, be-
comes "a blueprint for a kind of literary criticism designed
to promote social change."

Haddox, Thomas F. "Whitman's End of History: 'As I sat Alone
by Blue Ontario's Shore,' *Democratic Vistas*, and the Postbellum Politics of Nostalgia." *Walt Whitman Quarterly Review* 22 (Summer 2004), 1–22. Examines the 1867 poem
"As I sat Alone by Blue Ontario's Shore" and compares it
to its antebellum version ("Poem of Many In One") and to
Democratic Vistas, interrogating Whitman's "refusal to engage with the complexities of the present moment" as, with
"Hegelian logic," he "proposes the end of history in the rise
of the United States," conflating poet, people, and nation in

a kind of transcendence of history, a transcendence that is troubled (but not defeated) by the Civil War and the social unrest of the Reconstruction period.

Davis, Robert Leigh. "Democratic Vistas." In Donald D. Kummings, ed., *A Companion to Walt Whitman* (Malden, Massachusetts: Blackwell, 2006), 540–552. Offers an extended reading of *Democratic Vistas*, tracking "Whitman's culture 'programme,'" with its ambition to accomplish "nothing less than a 'mental-educational' revolution of consciousness, the opening of the American mind," including the calling forth of a new kind of "supple and self-conscious reader."

Hunnicutt, Benjamin Kline. "Walt Whitman's 'Higher Progress' and Shorter Work Hours." *Walt Whitman Quarterly Review* 26 (Fall 2008), 92–109. Analyzes *Democratic Vistas* (and other writings) to demonstrate that part of Whitman's conception of "higher progress" involved the attainment of freedom beyond basic necessities in order to gain "liberty's ultimate challenge"—for "citizens to fill the purest of freedoms with activities that were complete in themselves"; goes on to track Whitman's involvement in the movement to reduce working hours, increase leisure, and develop "labor-saving machines," all of which formed "the obvious practical link between increasing material wealth and 'higher progress'"; concludes by considering the influence of Whitman's "higher progress" on John Maynard Keynes and on economists and historians of labor over the past fifty years.

{ The Iowa Whitman Series }